ALSO BY MANUEL GRIEGO

This Side of Heaven

The Threat

The Clandestine Club

Retrieval, and Beyond

A Schizophrenic Way

Manuel Griego

authorHOUSE®

AuthorHouse™
1663 Liberty Drive
Bloomington, IN 47403
www.authorhouse.com
Phone: 1-800-839-8640

First published by AuthorHouse 11/21/2011

ISBN: 978-1-4670-4352-6 (sc)
ISBN: 978-1-4670-4351-9 (e)

Library of Congress Control Number: 2011917975

Printed in the United States of America

This Book is
Lovingly and Gratefully Dedicated

To My Loved Ones at Home

And if any man think that he knows anything,
he knows nothing yet as he ought to know.

--1 Corinthians 8:2

Foreword

At middle age Manuel met and married the love of his life but only after he had taken complete control of it. As an adolescent he was raised in a very large, very poor and typically dysfunctional family with seven sisters and three brothers. His father was a typical abusive alcoholic and his mother overworked and overburdened with family responsibilities allowing him to practically make his own rules of behavior. Despite many bad influences in his childhood he managed to stay on the right side of the law and even attain a couple of college degrees. It seemed that he was off and running with both hands on the wheel to what appeared to be a promising and bright future, only to begin experiencing symptoms he could not understand. At first he began just having feelings of guilt, insecurity and loneliness. Then his life began to derail when he started having feelings of extreme paranoia, then delusions quickly crept into his state of mind. Unwilling to admit he was having serious mental problems he continued on his way not knowing he only had one hand on the wheel and one eye on the road.

Only after several severe schizophrenic episodes and suicide attempts did he completely realize he was still sane enough to realize that he was almost insane. He took complete control of his life when he finally admitted that he was a chronic paranoid schizophrenic. Under proper medication and treatment he learned, before it was too late, that he could not beat the madness that comes with schizophrenia. His only hope was to deal with it. Today, he is happily married with two wonderful children and a beautiful wife thanks in part to the medication he takes diligently every day. This is his story about survival.

PREFACE

The times, places and events written of in this book are as true as the author can recall. The names of all characters in the book have been changed. Only the author of the newspaper article reprinted in the book and the name of the newspaper where article was written have not been changed. The names of all characters in the article itself have been changed.

CONTENTS

RETRIEVAL, AND BEYOND

- A Schizophrenic Way

I

SURVIVING SCHIZOPHRENIA

Janos is a little village in the middle of nowhere. To call it a hole in the wall would be an understatement because it's much less than that. This town is a three hour drive west of Juarez, Mexico on Highway 2 just south of the U.S. border. There are only one stop sign, one hotel that's open and two restaurants in Janos. At this 'one-horse town' the frequent trucker makes his pit stop and the very occasional traveler just pauses as he passes through. It's at this one-intersection outpost where Lena and I found ourselves on our honeymoon. What were we doing in this God-forsaken corner of the world? We didn't care- and it didn't make any difference either we only knew that we were together and that's all that mattered.

We rented a room on the second floor of the Hacienda

Hotel. The steel stairs to the second floor were shaky, uneven and much steeper than normal stairs. If one didn't grab on to the rail there would surely be an accident and a law suit waiting to be had. That is the thought that went through my mind as we climbed the stairs- but of course we were in Mexico, so if one of us was to fall and have an unfortunate accident we'd just have to suffer through the consequences. We only left our room without a view when we absolutely had to- for food, and that was only once a day.

Nevertheless, this small place was busy and noisy all night and day. It seemed like there were 18 wheelers every half hour round the clock stopping for fuel or whatever else the truckers needed. What made it worse was that it seemed like none of them had mufflers. We made the best of it though. We didn't care about the noise, the cold running water or the cheap wine we were drinking. It was February and we had plenty of blankets, love and laughter to keep us entertained for the three days and nights we spent in Janos, Mexico. The very snowy, three-channel television without a remote control only added to the ambiance.

For me, it had been about three years. From the moment I set my eyes on Lena I had decided to wait. And I did! I was determined that everything had to be done right this time. After all, one doesn't run into the love of his life everyday- it only happens once in a lifetime and I was wise enough to recognize it. I would do nothing to ruin an opportunity to be happy and fulfilled at the same time.

For her, it had been over five years. There had only been one other man in her life- her first husband and he was abusive to her in every way but physical. During her pregnancy he often left her cold and hungry while he was off with his other conquests. Her weekly food allowance was fifty pesos- at the time about six dollars. When I met her she was thirty two years old and very proud not to have been in any other relationship besides her first marriage. After what she went through with Lalo she was determined not to get involved with another man. Their relationship had soured so much that shortly after her daughter Diana was born he was going to leave them at a local S-Mart. The store was quite a distance from her parent's house, but she made him take her to the front door of her parent's home. When Lena and Diana got home they of course were taken in. One day her ex-husband unexpectedly showed up at her place of work, but Lena didn't see him or talk to him because as far as she was concerned he didn't really care about his own daughter much less her. Lalo never made an effort to see Diana, or help support her as he had agreed to in the divorce decree. After Lena divorced him she was determined to raise Diana on her own. She was also determined not to have anything to do with another man, ever, but fortunately I was able to convince her otherwise.

We met through an uncle of hers. At the time I had a brother that was very depressed because he was going through a very bad divorce and he had a friend, Miguel that he worked with who invited him to go night-clubbing in Juarez. My brother told me they were going to party in Mexico and I decided to tag along. It is a four hour drive from Albuquerque to Juarez and on the way Miguel was telling me about his niece, Lena. I was curious to know this single mother raising a child on her own in Mexico. It's difficult enough for a single mother to raise a child in the United States but in Mexico, it must be exceedingly more difficult. Her Uncle Miguel told me she was a good worker, stayed at home and never ran around with other men. That alone made me so curious that I wanted to meet her. I had known a few other women in my life, but as it was, none of them needed me- I mean really needed me. It seemed to me that she might need a man to help take care of her and her child. The only thing I needed to do was to make her fall in love with me and I had no idea if that was going to be easy or impossible, but I sure was going to try.

Once I met her she seemed, at least on the surface, to be everything her uncle described. She was tall, slim with long brown hair and green eyes and a pleasant but cautious demeanor. I waited about three months to make contact with her again as I dropped in on her at her father's home without prior notice. To my good fortune she was not home. She was in Chihuahua, Mexico visiting her cousins. That gave me the opportunity to talk with her father about my intentions, which of course were genuine. He was impressed because I did not do much talking as my Spanish was not very good but I was able to get the point across that I wanted to get to know his daughter. We briefly talked by phone and she vaguely remembered me but was willing to give me a chance to visit with her when she returned from Chihuahua. We met again, officially, a month later and agreed to communicate occasionally by phone and periodically in person. It eventually came to be that I was making the trip to Juarez monthly on weekends. We got to know each other very well and after about a year and a half of making many trips to Mexico I asked her to marry me, and she said yes.

How we ended up in Janos I'm not quite sure, all I know is that we left the wedding chapel in Palomas, Mexico and drove west on Highway 2 until we got tired of driving. Why we didn't honeymoon in the States is because she did not have a VISA to enter the U.S. and I didn't want to wait for her to get one so we decided to get married anyway. We were married but separated as she was temporarily living in Juarez and I was permanently living in Albuquerque. I continued making monthly trips until Lena and her daughter got temporary Green Cards. At last count it was over 40 trips from Albuquerque to Juarez in my very dependable 1996 Acura.

As it is now, we live happily in the Albuquerque, New Mexico area. Besides her daughter we have a three year old son of our own who is in all manner and form perfect. What does all of this have to do with surviving schizophrenia? Well, I am a chronic paranoid schizophrenic and for many years have suffered from this illness. How I arrived where I am now could be of importance to others living with schizophrenia being that I suffered for many, many years through many, many schizophrenic episodes to be where I am now- happy, fulfilled and successful. It is my hope that this story (which is as true as I can recall), will give some insight to the illness and how I am able to successfully live with it. It is unlikely that I will reveal anything new about schizophrenia but the struggle to overcome the obstacles of living with it could offer someone, somewhere out there, the armor to daily deal with this cruel, cruel mental disorder. It's not known exactly what brings on the illness. I've been told it's hereditary, but there is no one anywhere in my extended family as far as I can tell that has ever suffered from schizophrenia. Maybe there is a hint in my childhood how it came about so here I loosely write about my upbringing. In my case however, I believe that stress is the obvious instigator. It's not possible to completely rid oneself of the disease because it is chronic, but to learn about the tools I use to live with it and lead a normal and active life can be rewarding. This is what I hope others can gain from reading this book- some of the skills that I use to cope with schizophrenia daily.

II

CHILDHOOD

To be born into a poor family one would think that from that day life begins at a disadvantage, and that all the necessities of life come through a much more difficult road because the means to provide are scant. The effort 'to provide' is more exhaustive because more effort is spent required simply to survive, but when social classes are blurred at an early age being rich or poor is sometimes inconsequential. That's the way it was with me. I was born into a very large family with very thin financial resources. I was fortunate enough to be the fifth of eleven siblings. Even though we were poor, it didn't necessarily inhibit me from the same opportunities that the rich had. At least in our small community the rich ran as easily with the poor as the poor with the poor and the rich with the rich. Classes were either completely blurred, or as children we simply didn't care. I don't know which. What I do recall is that most of the time life as a child was very good. Occasionally there were hard times but they were few and far between. I always had enough to eat with clothes on my back and shoes on my feet and when the basics are fulfilled as a child everything else seems almost irrelevant.

The front door of our green five room house was just ten yards away from the famed Route 66, and the back door was about a hundred yards away from the AT&SF railroad tracks. We had one restroom, one tub, one sink and one table for all thirteen family members. Yes, there were seven girls and four boys in our family. One can only imagine what it was like around the kitchen table during meals. There were a lot of hungry faces reaching for the potatoes, or beans, or bread, or whatever it was we were eating. I don't remember ever walking away hungry. Worried about where the next meal was coming from yes, as I was once asked my mother and she quickly answered, "God will provide so don't worry." After that, I kept my mouth shut, and my mouth full.

Living on Highway 66 made many smart businessmen rich and my father also tried to tap into that gold mine. To the west of our little green house he built a string of ten, one bedroom apartments that he rented to supplement his miner's income. Yes, my father was a miner. As I recall he mined a lot of things- like coal, uranium and fluorspar. During most of the time I was at home he mined uranium. As for the apartments- that never worked out because the renters very early in the morning would steal the sheets and pillows and everything else that was not tied down. They eventually served as bedrooms for me and my older brother because the main house was much too small for all of us.

Grants was the name of the small mining town where we lived. It was located near the mid-northwest part of New Mexico. The townspeople there often bragged that Grants was the "Uranium Capital of the World." Those who lived there worked in the mines, were related to, or knew someone who worked in them. If you graduated from the local high school chances were you would become a miner like your father, uncle or friend. Unless you completely left Grants to bigger and better places life was simple and work physically was very hard. I learned this early in my life when I took on a summertime job as a miner's helper at one of the local mines.

My older brother and I would sleep in the 'abandoned' apartments and depending on what time of year it was would determine in which room we slept. In the summer we slept in Room 5 because it was cooler than any other of the rooms and in the winter we slept in Room 1 because it had a wood stove. One night, as I was sleeping in Room 5 alone it got a little cold and there was no electricity in the rooms so I rigged up a source of heat for myself. I ran an electrical cord from the main house to the room, then tied the cord with a light bulb to the ceiling light fixture and placed the light under the blanket making a lighted tent for myself and then fell asleep. Early the next morning I woke up in a room full of smoke with the cotton mattress burning under me. Fortunately only the blanket and mattress burned and it smoked for days and days out back.

On certain weekends, when our father had a long weekend, most of us would climb into the family car and drive to

Albuquerque- about 75 miles away. In those days gas was very, very inexpensive and with $2.00 of gasoline we could drive all the way to Albuquerque to visit my grandmother on my mother's side. On one trip our parents thought everyone was in the car so we left for Grants and didn't realize until we were well on our way that one or our sisters was left behind. Naturally we went back for her.

III

LIFE WITH FATHER

The role of any father is to guide and support his family so that his children can become productive members of society. His role is to worry about the welfare of his children and make sure he does all he can to provide them with love and security. Unfortunately, not all fathers no matter how hard they try are capable of meeting these obligations. Our father, as far as I'm concerned, sometimes fell short of these obligations. My purpose in this chapter is not to tear him down as he is gone and unable to defend himself, but will be to expose some of his character as I saw it. My siblings can write their own book and express what they feel about our father in their own way.

Our father was not always a loving, caring parent. Though he did for the most part provide us with food and clothing and shelter there were times when we had to provide for ourselves. As I remember, when my older sisters were old enough to work they did so for their own benefit and because our father couldn't always provide sufficiently for their personal needs. They worked and bought some of their own clothes, paid for their own lunches at school and provided means for their own entertainment. As for me, I too worked at various jobs trying to earn some money for my personal needs- like athletics. At the age of twelve the very first job I ever had was pulling weeds one day at a local motel for a quarter. At the local theatre I worked nights to make a little money. I played basketball and ran track in junior high and high school and always needed athletic equipment. On many occasions I had to borrow shoes to run track and play football. Because I was an athlete, my time was taken up practicing the sport I was in and didn't have time to work so I couldn't always buy the things I needed. I was dependent mostly on borrowing, and unfortunately, stealing some of the things I needed. Of course, that was my own doing and my father never knew.

It is difficult to admit, but our father often was a typical abusive, alcoholic miner. With me he was only verbally abusive, but there were a couple of times when he punished me for no reason at all. There was one instance when I was walking home from my friend's house and as I walked in the door he was waiting with a belt that he used on me several times. I still don't know why. His verbal abuse was often excessive especially when he had been drinking. He would tell me some things I would rather not repeat, but are stored in my memory so clearly as if he was telling me right now.

To my older brother and two younger brothers he was not

only verbally abusive but he was also physically abusive. I remember one evening at the dinner table after everyone had finished eating my younger brother was sitting at the table next to our very drunk father. For reasons known only to him he grabbed my brother by the hair and repeatedly pounded his head against the brick wall behind him. I could never understand what my brother could have done to deserve such abuse because he was only about ten or eleven years old at the time. I saw this and went into the living room and told our mother what he was doing and she told me to tell our father she wants to talk to my brother and he very reluctantly let him go.

To my older brother he was especially mean and abusive. As the oldest son, I assume our father expected him to be special. My brother had a mind of his own and generally did what he wanted when he wanted. He had a very wild streak in him as well, and our father knew this. On one occasion he and a couple of friends ditched school in our father's tan 1958 Chevy Pickup. They went up to Mt. Taylor, a twenty minute dirt-road drive from Grants. My brother loved to drive fast and didn't know that speed and gravel roads don't mix. On the way up the mountain the truck began to fishtail out of control and it flipped a couple of times down a shallow cliff. Fortunately the truck landed on its wheels and except for a few bumps and bruises they were all uninjured. According to their reaction after the accident all they had done was miss a day of school.

Our father, however, was devastated. To see his shiny, well cared-for truck all banged up made him so angry that he took it out on everyone. The first thing he did was look for my older brother because he knew right away exactly what had happened. My brother was nowhere to be found and the next day he left the truck at home and went to football practice with bruises and all.

To this day I don't know if it was for ditching school or for the wrecked truck but our father went in the banged up truck for my brother and literally yanked him straight out of football practice uniform and all. On the way home I was sitting in the middle, and our father repeatedly reached over me to strike my brother with the back of his hand. He fiercely backhanded him again and again until both my father's hand and my brother's teeth were bleeding. When we finally got home the lectures and the verbal abuse began. That night and for days after, my father hovered over my brother just waiting for him to make another mistake. There's no telling what he would have done to him if he would have done something wrong again. Years later I can recall one of my brothers front teeth turning gray and it was probably because of the beating he had taken in high school.

On winter nights my brother and I would sleep in Room 1 where there was the wood stove. As it was in winter time when the nights were very cold we would start a fire at the beginning of the night but we were too lazy to get up from under the warm blankets to put another log in the stove. Our father knew this so he would come from the main house just to get the fire going again and also to lecture my brother for an hour or two in the process.

Much of the time, however, our father was not around. He worked days, nights or the swing shift. If he wasn't working the day shift he was sleeping or passed out in his bedroom on weekends. When he was home he was very intimidating.

Many times when I was with him he took me to a bar and left me outside waiting for him in the truck for hours. Sometimes, if he wasn't too drunk he would bring me out a bag of peanuts.

As you might imagine the drive home was very interesting. Sometimes we wondered how he ever made it to the house. On one occasion he was in my brother-in-law's yellow, 1957 Ford Fairlane, and you guessed it- he totaled it. He was so drunk he hit a parked car from behind then he got in a physical scuffle with a policeman and ripped the policeman's jacket to pieces. My older brother happened to be driving by at that instant and in defense of our drunken father, joined into the scuffle with the policeman. I don't recall how they got out of that mess but it was not unusual for my father to spend a night in jail.

Physically, he was not a big person but he made up for his size with his aggressive nature. Being a miner he was extremely strong and from his stocky, brusque build came a very deep forceful voice. When he wanted to say something there was no doubt about him getting his point across. He came from a family of miners. He had two, much older brothers who died months apart in, or because of the mines. One of his younger brothers was about thirty six years old when he suffered a serious accident in the mines and was crippled for life. He eventually died at an elderly age from his injuries. My father often would proudly declare, "I spent twenty nine years and seven months underground to keep you fed and clothed and a roof over your head, and I don't have to be your father I do it because I want to not because I have to."

IV

COMRADES IN CRIME

Impressionable and long lasting influences at a young age often determine the direction a boy will take and the ultimate road that he chooses. If two people come from essentially the same background it is impossible to know who will fail and who will succeed in the game of life. I do not use the word 'game' lightly because life certainly is not a game. It's more of a journey through good, bad, neutral and meaningless experiences. The 'boy' able to consistently interpret a positive result from his wide range of experiences will more likely succeed, and the 'boy' unable to consistently respond positively to his experiences will most likely fail. What I mean by 'positively' is: a reaction to an experience where an individual gains some wisdom or knowledge in order to ease the impact of the next unknown experience whether it is good, bad, neutral or meaningless. To follow in this chapter are two individuals from essentially the same background but one considers himself a success in life and the other as you will see is a failure in every way.

As a child I had a friend and neighbor and his name was Ray. Together we were a terror to the whole town of Grants. Ray was two years my senior and he had a profound influence on my childhood and teen years. I knew him from as far back as I can remember because he lived next door. Ray had two brothers and two sisters and his father was a mechanic and drove a wrecker and his mother was a housewife. From about the age of twelve I can remember strongly being under his influence. Together we were fearless comrades. At that age I didn't know clearly the difference between right and wrong. I was always ready and willing to follow his lead because he was older and more experienced than me. If he got an idea to do something illegal I wouldn't hesitate for one second to join him in his mischief and he was always looking to cause some trouble to someone somewhere. I was just what he needed- a sidekick to boss around and impress. For example, if either of us needed a part for our bicycle (that we couldn't afford to buy) we would just steal it, and our bikes were tickets to our adventures and our transportation to anywhere in Grants we wanted to go.

As we rode around on our bikes, usually after dark, Ray would always carry a bottle opener so he could pop the top off any soft drink from those old-fashioned coke machines whenever he got thirsty. Coke machines were easy to find because they were conspicuously located all over the city. Using a straw or small cup we could drink as much soda of whatever flavor we wanted until we were full. If we needed money Ray knew where his hard-working older brother would hide his stash and would raid it. His older brother, Jimmy knew this of course, and when he got a hold of Ray he would physically beat the hell out of him. Ray could take a beating like no one I ever knew after all he had survived his mother's beatings for years.

When we were bored and had nothing to do, Ray would come up with the sneakiest schemes for us to have a good time. One day we were trying to figure out a way to impress Laura- the girl next door. Ray told me that she loved horses but if we took his brothers horses that would be the end of him. So, he told me he knew where there were some loose horses that didn't belong to anyone that we could ride. Off we went on old Route 66 past Mount Taylor Park for those horses so we could take Laura for a ride. It took us all day to catch those damn horses because they were loose. We chased them for hours until we finally cornered them half way up the mesa against the barb wire fence. The two horses we roped were very tame and probably very old otherwise we wouldn't have been able to corner them so with our makeshift bridles. We steered them down Old 66 thinking Laura was going to love this. We didn't make it to her house because the police caught us first. As close as we got was right in front of my Aunt Jodie's house on Route 66 about two blocks from my house. "Where did you get these horses? Whose horses are they? What are you doing riding them into town? Who's your dad?" The policeman asked me. He didn't even bother asking Ray a single question- he simply put him in the back seat of the police car because he already knew who Ray was. To this day I can see Ray sitting there in the back seat of that police car pointing at me and laughing because I had to stand there between the two horses holding them with those makeshift bridles. Finally, my mother came and slapped me across the face asking me what the hell was I doing stealing horses? "Just you wait till your father gets home," She said.

It turned out the horses did belong to someone, of course-the Grants School Superintendent, Mr. McMann. Was he ever pissed off when he showed up to claim his horses! "Where the hell did you cut my fences you little bastard?" He screamed at me. I told him we didn't cut the fences we just separated the barbwires halfway up the mesa and pulled them through the fence. He then rode off in the dark sitting on one horse and leading the other one behind him with the same rope we had used as a bridle.

Ray was released in his father's custody and I was placed in a jail cell. I sat there for half the night on a cold steel bunk bed looking out through the jailhouse bars of the basement window at the cars passing by on old Route 66. My father, after he got off his graveyard shift, picked me up and I presume also bailed me out of jail that night. It turned out they had locked me up in that jail cell just to scare me straight because I was only twelve years old at the time. I'm not sure but I think it might have worked. Considering what my father could have done, he actually let me off easy. He thought it was funny and at that time needed something to cheer him up because he had just lost two older brothers.

Ray's rebellious nature continued and I personally think it was because it was a reaction to his mother's abusive discipline. Instead of trying to teach him to stay out of trouble she drove him to deliberately commit more. As punishment she would force him to make adobes in the backyard during the blistering summer heat and in the freezing winter cold, and I think it was for no other reason than plain old meanness. I realized this because those adobes lay there unused for years. Whenever Ray did something wrong or whenever she felt like it to the backyard to make adobes he would go. As far as I could tell Ray's father was as passive as any father could be. He seemed to be completely intimidated by her and maybe even afraid of that mean old lady. Ray always gave his overbearing mother a reason to punish him. He was always looking for trouble and almost always finding it- at home or on the streets. The last I heard Ray was in prison for raping a fifty year old lady that he threatened to rape again if she said anything. He did his time for that crime but is now in a New Mexico State Prison for tossing gasoline on a neighbor and setting him on fire because his neighbor was leaning on his fence. This I know because it was all over TV on the evening local news.

Why he is where he is and why I am where I am is a mystery that is beyond anyone to understand considering that we both came from essentially the same background. Obviously, his response to the good, bad, neutral and meaningless experiences in life was not as positive as mine. He apparently did not gain any useful wisdom or knowledge from his bad experiences and continued on the same old road that ultimately led him to failure. I do mean failure in every sense of the word.

V

EXPRESSIONS OF PATERNAL LOVE

A father is likely to raise well-balanced children if he can consistently, openly and honestly express his love for them. His affection is more important than any material things. Objects are always temporal, but a demonstration of true and sincere affection is permanent. A vehicle, for example, given to a son or daughter as a form of love is surely appreciated but cannot replace the sense of security, trust and self-assuredness that comes with genuine love. Material objects can help children negotiate through the certain challenges they encounter everyday but in time are replaceable. Being raised with security, trust, and love are not negotiable- they drive the core of a persons being. They provide the tools to handle whatever situation one may encounter. What a father with sincere expressions of love for his offspring provides is beyond measure. A secure and self-assured individual will actually provide for him or herself much sooner than an individual who has to develop those qualities on his or her own. I personally spent many, many years believing myself to be self-assured and secure only to find I was insecure and unable to trust or love.

There were a few rare tender moments I can remember that I shared with my father but I didn't even know enough to recognize them when they did happen. Sometimes, when he was sober, I think, he would hug me and lift me up in the air and this was his way of physically showing his affection. This behavior was so rare and so peculiar I didn't know how to accept it so I would gently push him away. I didn't know if he was sincere or if it was his drinking and this caused me to be suspicious not only of him and his behavior but of practically everyone- male or female.

One way he demonstrated his interest and concern for me was when he offered to take me and my brothers hunting with him. My father loved to take us hunting. He was a very good hunter because he always knew where and when to find deer. For example, he knew there were always deer near an old mining camp where he had worked as a young man. On one particular hunting season we went to the Zuni Mountains to that old camp sight very early in the morning. As the sun rose we turned the bend on that old mountain road near the abandoned mineshaft and we spotted several deer. He quickly picked one out, shot it from the open truck window and bang- we had one! It was a six point buck!

I jumped out of the truck and ran toward the wounded deer as fast as I could and grabbed him by the horns. He was still jerking fiercely and moving his head back and forth and up and down. My father had hit him in the spine and it was unable to move its two back legs. While there still was a lot of life in the front half of the deer my father stabbed its heart with a big knife and it quickly died. We hung it from a large tree branch and dressed it to take home. He had killed the first deer of the hunting season and we were so excited that we didn't bother to tag it with the license. It was barely daybreak when he shot the deer and we were home within the hour. On the way home there was no checkpoint so we innocently drove home without ever tagging the deer.

Later that evening my father and my older brother went back to the Zuni Mountains to hunt another deer. And wouldn't you know- they got another one. Unfortunately this one was a doe. It was a huge female deer and that was illegal so they concocted a scheme to take the deer home. What they did was hide it under a large tree near some bushes so that no one would see it or take it. Then they went home without the doe and cut off the head of the buck he had killed that morning and took it back with them. What they planned was to bring back the doe with the head of the buck at night so no one would know the difference if there was a checkpoint, and there was. The Ranger, however, was more prepared than they imagined. He got suspicious when he saw the head separated from the body and investigated the deer very closely. So close that he realized what they had done. That little venture for the second deer cost my father his new 30-30 Winchester rifle, a $300 fine, both deer, and an appearance before the judge.

Everyone who knew my father generally knew him as a very mean man. He was very strict with his four sons not to mention his seven daughters. But he also had a courageous side. One evening there was a wildly rabid dog that had everyone in the neighborhood running scared- especially all the kids. Someone had earlier called the dog pound and the dogcatchers came but when they saw how big and vicious the dog was they were too frightened to get close to the sick dog. The dog definitely had rabies and it just kept coming closer and closer to our little green brick house until it finally rested under my father's yellow Dodge. Someone had to take control as the dogcatchers had no spine. Unlike in <u>To Kill a Mockingbird</u> where Atticus Finch shoots the rabid dog from a fair distance, my father couldn't shoot because there were houses and people and cars all around. What he did was to take the restraining- pole with the rope attached to the end of it from the dogcatchers and collar the dog himself. He then proceeded to pick the dog up with the pole and tossed it into the dogcatcher's cage in back of the pickup. Then, in a fit of anger he ran off the cowardly dogcatchers.

There was one other instance where I recall seeing just how courageous he could be. Behind our little green house was a small open field where I had set my basketball goal and behind it was a wrecking yard. There were about thirty or forty wrecked cars that were lined up in such a way the neighborhood kids could often play the game of tag jumping from car to car. Sometimes we would break off the metal trim from the sides of the cars and make swords to compete in our own form of medieval sword fights. I still have a six inch scar on the right side of my chest to attest to these battles. Anyway, sometimes the neighborhood kids took out the back seats from the cars to jump up and down on them just for fun. On this occasion I heard a rattling noise under the car seat every time I jumped down on it. Someone told my father about this and he came and turned the car seat over where he found a live rattle snake. My father went for a shovel and immediately killed it with the shovel.

My father was proud to be a miner and would often take me or my brothers with him to the mines. He did not want us to be miners because he knew how hard and dangerous that kind of work was. I believe he wanted us to experience for ourselves exactly what it was to be a miner. I went into one of the mines where he worked and quickly saw for myself how dangerous it was and how easy it was for someone to get hurt or even killed in a mine. I often wonder how he survived twenty nine years and seven months underground in those mines. One weekend he told us that it would be too dangerous for anyone to go in so he closed the mine that weekend. That very weekend the mineshaft caved in and that mine became so dangerous that it was completely shut down.

When my father could no longer pass the required physical to be a miner, and as he put it, was 'thrown out' of mining completely. That meant he had no means of supporting his family. So he went to work for smaller independent mining companies. The only way they would let him work was if he signed a waiver relieving them of any responsibility for his health.

Though my father was unable or unwilling to completely and consistently demonstrate the fact that he truly did love us, in his own way he tried to give us love and security the only way he knew. Unfortunately because his drinking got in the way of almost everything, we all suffered and some of us more than others. Now, as a parent myself, I know that I was not given support and affection when a child. Partly because of that, I was in turn unable to love or trust others. Most of my relationships were completely empty or shallow and I would inadvertently hurt others without knowing and I needed almost a lifetime to get over my insecurities. Today, I am self-assured and confident about what I do and where I'm going and in what direction I lead my family.

VI

OUT OF CONTROL

When a father loses control it is generally because he is way over his head in family problems and has become overwhelmed with his circumstance. This is what happened along the way with my father. There were hints of his lack of control, when in one particular instance he overreacted. One evening Ray and I were riding Chocolate (the tamest and oldest of Ray's brother's horses) and as my father drove into the backyard his headlights apparently spooked the horse and we were both bucked off the horse. Not only were we thrown off Chocolate, but my father kicked me in the butt a few times with his steel-toed boots just for being on a horse. He told me that will be the last time he wants to see me on any of those horses ever again. It was the last time he saw me on the horse, but not the last time I rode them.

It was a complete mystery what drove my father to do some of the things he did. I mean, there were times when he was completely out of control. For instance, in order to support his family he had to work and in order to work in the mines he had to pass a routine physical. He went for a physical with Dr. Garcia and the good doctor couldn't give him a clean bill of health. Dad flunked the exam. That, of course meant that he couldn't work which meant he couldn't support his family. He subsequently threatened the doctor with a pocketknife. I don't know the extent of the conversation that followed in the doctor's office but the fact that he pulled a knife out on the doctor became common knowledge. There were also other incidents which revealed just how wild my father could get.

I knew of another pocketknife incident even more serious that could have cost a complete stranger serious injury, maybe even his life. One of my younger sisters was working for a boss who refused to pay her what she was owed. She had worked a few weeks for this man and was due a paycheck which her boss refused to give. She told our father about this man who refused to pay her and he immediately drove to her former place of employment. While holding his pocketknife to her boss' throat Dad verbally threatened him. The six hundred dollar check he wrote to my sister cleared the bank without incident.

As far as I knew he never physically abused any of his seven daughters but there were things he made them do they won't forget. He once met and befriended a complete stranger in a bar and together they made plans to go partying. My father went home and picked up one of my older sisters and took her to this man's trailer house so she could babysit the stranger's children. My father left her there babysitting complete strangers while they went off to party. Eventually my father went home alone and completely forgot about my sister. The stranger finally came staggering into the trailer at dawn only to find my sister sitting on the couch petrified and crying. He actually left her there alone with that stranger not knowing where she was or how she was going to get home. Fortunately the man drove her home without any problems.

Our father, I hate to admit, had his favorites. There were eleven of us and I for one avoided the man as much as possible because I knew he could be unpredictable when he was drinking. I believe I was on his good side because he rarely ever found reason to physically beat or verbally abuse me. The two oldest were the most rebellious of all of us. Our oldest sister and our father never saw eye to eye on anything. They were always arguing about anything and everything. Our oldest brother also rarely saw a moment of peace.

(It is difficult to admit just how out of control our father got. He actually physically attacked our youngest brother with the same pocketknife he used to threaten others. As I was told, my father actually drew blood. If my older brother hadn't walked in at that very moment it could have been disastrous. These 'out of control' incidents were years apart so it's possible that he could have gone out of control at any time. The worst my father ever did to me was hurt my feelings by crapping in the front of my basketball goal one night when he thought I wasn't around.

His natural disposition, most of the time, was just plain old anger especially when he was drinking. I recall one night that he came home so drunk he purposely crapped all over the living room floor and one of my sisters had to clean it up. I can understand why he was always so angry. He lived a very hard life spending much of it underground sucking dirt to support eleven kids, but that was his own doing. He and my mother, from the moment they met, decided to have as many kids as they could. He told me this himself. No matter the economics, no matter how hard things got, no matter who got hurt, no matter anything- they were determined to live their lives the way they had planned. Of course, they did not know what lay ahead when they met and married- they only knew that they were going to live their lives the way they wanted and they surely did.

VII

A MOTHER'S COHERANCE

For one parent to be practically negligent in the upbringing of the children in the family is a terrible predicament for any family to live in. For the other parent to be overwhelmed with responsibilities makes the situation even worse. Imagine, an often absent and abusive alcoholic father on the one hand and on the other a mother that is so submerged in the nurturing and chores of the family. It is a wonder how our family ever survived. I can clearly remember when our father and mother argued. They argued about the tiniest little detail and would blow it up like it was the end of the world. They argued about each other's families, about money, about his drinking and just about anything they could think of. When they really got going they would argue in Spanish. I never saw my father hit my mother but

I was told he once held a gun to her face. I don't know if that is true but I wouldn't doubt it for a minute. How they were ever able to have eleven children together is beyond me because they very rarely showed any signs of real love or affection for each other.

Our family was a classic dysfunctional family that in every way survived on a shoe string. The older members of the family helped take care of the younger ones and the ones in the middle (like me) somehow just managed to remain alive. Not all eleven of us made it out alive. One of my younger brothers (my mother's favorite child) died from injuries in a motorcycle accident when he was just seventeen and, my older brother committed suicide about four years later when he was twenty eight. What he did was put a rifle under his chin and pull the trigger. It's been more than four decades since those childhood days in Grants. I'm sure some of my siblings suffered more than others and I hope most of their scars have healed. In my case, I don't hold any resentment towards our parents for having raised us the way they did. On the other hand, I feel fortunate to have lived through that childhood because I now know what not to let happen to my own family.

In those days, our mother held things together for all of us. She kept some sort of sanity in the house and that was an enormous job. From the oldest to the youngest and everyone in between she made that situation coherent. While our father provided the financial means for us to survive she provided the glue that held us together. She did the cooking, cleaning, sweeping, and washing- whatever needed to be done she did it, with the help of course of my older sisters. Without her nothing would have gotten done. The only thing she couldn't do enough of was to nurture each of the eleven children adequately. That was understandable and for the most part, we all had to share what little of our mother's love and affection we could get.

She was overwhelmed with ten other kids to rear she just had no time for me personally. As I recall it seemed as if she always had a baby in her arms not to mention her household responsibilities. On top of everything else she had to contend with a mean, argumentative, alcoholic husband whenever he was home. I imagine the rest of my siblings must have felt the same way at some time during those dreadful days. Survival as a child without a mother's love was a personal thing and each us dealt with it in our own way. In other words, for the most part, we lived practically without it.

I don't blame my mother for not being able to love me adequately when I was a child because she gave what she could, as much as she could when she could. She was as loving as possible considering the circumstances. In fact, I can't remember ever getting a hug or a kiss from my mother when I was a child. She was too busy just to take time for me and I know now that affected me for many, many years. I had no idea for those many years that the proper nurturing of a child has to affect a person's growth as a human being. My growth, as far as relationships with others, was always stunted because I didn't know how to connect with people.

VIII

HIGH SCHOOL YEARS

In our world, success is generally measured financially. Even the dictionaries define success as the gaining of wealth or fame. Financial success is most easily recognized because people are always ready and willing to show their ability to acquire. The most obvious demonstration of a person's success is in the neighborhood where one lives. Fame, too, is obviously always out there. The dictionaries also say that success is 'the satisfactory completion of something.' My junior high and high school years allowed me to personally experience success on a relatively small scale. What follows in this chapter is a brief account of those years and the conclusion of my experience with fame at a relatively small scale and the successful completion of what to me at the time was a major accomplishment.

Entering the 7th grade for me was almost a Godsend because what I left behind would eventually have led me in a direction of total failure. In the first place I hooked up with friends who, like me, had an interest in athletics. Leaving behind my delinquent behavior was not at all that easy, because there were also young troublemakers that I met and briefly associated with. There were some characters as early as the 8th grade that were driving cars and carrying guns and knives to school. They had obviously been left back a grade or two and had learned the system. They knew what they could get away with and tested it to the limit. Cesar was one of those individuals that had a full beard and mustache in the 8th grade and we of course being a little younger were impressed and influenced by his maturity. He along with Paul did temporarily have some influence on me. Paul and I would stay out late practically every night and with no parent to discipline me I had the freedom to run around as I pleased. We'd go about stealing things, breaking windows, sneaking into movies, breaking into and vandalizing schools and many other juvenile delinquent things. What eventually became of him I don't know as I lost touch with Paul as quickly as I got to know him.

At the very young age of thirteen I had to make a decision about which road I was going to hoe the rest of my life. I didn't know it at the time of course because I didn't know the difference or didn't care about the difference between right and wrong. With influences pulling on me from both sides of the street it was up to me and only me to decide. Fortunately, I was very gradually being led into the lawful and right side of the road. By the time I was seventeen I was firmly, though not yet completely, a righteous kind of guy.

In the 7th grade I joined the basketball team at Franklin Jr. High and even made the starting five. We won our share of games and I especially enjoyed the road trips and the camaraderie between athletes. This was something completely new to me and I liked it. In the 8th grade I made the varsity and even played with the 9th graders. And of course, there were the cheerleaders- they too had an impact on helping to change and shape my character. Brenda, my on again- off again girlfriend, was a cheerleader that told me once basketball was more important to me than her. She put me to the test and I foolishly fell for it. We had a curfew imposed on us by our coach, Mr. Riley. Cheerleaders of course had no curfews. I stayed past curfew one night with her and was subsequently suspended for a couple of games. She, on the other hand, went to the games that I couldn't go to. Needless to say our future as a couple, from the beginning, was limited. As I learned later she actually never had an interest in me. Why she even pretended to be my girlfriend to this day I have no idea. I never clearly got to know what her motives were in using me as she did. It was in her best interest to keep me close but as things turned out that did not happen.

In the 8th grade I added football to my athletic activities and made the defensive starting team. I was the right side linebacker. As a team we were all very small and as a linebacker I was even tiny. So small were we that as a rule our coach, Mr. Medina, had the linebackers literally push the lineman into the offense when the ball was hiked. We were told to put both hands on the guards behind and push him as hard as we can into action as soon as the ball was hiked. On one occasion I jumped the gun and caused the lineman to be called for being off-sides. I paid for this with five swats with a wood paddle from the coach when we got to the locker room after the game. In those days it was legal to use corporal punishment and in those days it often worked.

In addition to basketball and football I added track to my athletic repertoire in the 9th grade. The 440 relay, 660 run and the high jump were my specialties. As a 9th grader I was asked by Mr. Grier, the high school coach to run the 880 during the district track meet. If I had come in at least 5th in the district meet I would have lettered but I finished 7th. As a football player I was promoted to running back and even made one touchdown. I had a habit of fumbling the football. I would fumble at least once in every game so my coach made me carry a football with me everywhere I went the week before we were to play our hated cross town rivals-Webster Jr. High. We won that game 13-6 and I scored a touchdown and didn't fumble! As for basketball we won more than we lost and I clearly remember scoring 31 points in one game though I don't recall who it was against. I left junior high with various letters and a number of ribbons for track and feeling quite proud of myself.

As a sophomore my athletic skills continued to grow. I tried every sport until I finally found one at which I could excel. Football was much too aggressive and eating dirt wasn't for me as we practiced on a dirt field. Besides, I didn't have the size to succeed at it. At the time I was too slow for track, baseball was not that popular and tennis was not that well organized. There was not even a soccer team at our high school to join and wrestling required much too much training and the benefit wasn't worth it. So basketball it was. I could train on my own in my own backyard and could often find a pickup game to practice my skills. Though I did go out for football I lasted only a week on the team because I just didn't like eating dirt and I ate a lot. I had decided to concentrate on basketball because it came natural to me and I could jump. At a mere 5' 9" I was able to very easily grab the rim. I couldn't dunk yet but I could shoot over practically anyone. When in Jr. High I remembered that the High School had qualified for the state tournament but they lost in the first round to Silver City. That seemed to me like a reasonable goal to set for myself- to make the state tournament and win at least one game. That was something that our high school had never done.

I made the varsity as a sophomore but got very little playing time. If I did play it was when we were very far ahead and very late in the game but I didn't play enough to letter. I finished the 10th grade without a letter and I don't even remember if I ran track that year. My junior year was another story as an athlete and as a student. Behind me were my delinquency days, at least, I thought. One of my cohorts easily convinced me to skip school one day and was caught ditching by my coach. Again I had been suspended for a couple of basketball games. This time it wasn't because of a girl it was because of a friend that I thought was a friend.

As a junior I was involved in various school activities. I was a member of the School Spirit Troops- it was something like a club that policed the school. Yes, me a rank amateur police assistant. I was a member of the student council and was also elected as Mr. Junior and even ran for student council vice-president and won. That meant that as a senior I was going to be the student council vice-president. Someone I know now I was not qualified to be. It was all a question of popularity and that at the time I certainly had plenty of recognition. How I got talked into running for vice-president I am not quite sure, I only know that it happened and there I was.

My basketball career as a junior was quite an improvement over my sophomore year. I made the starting team and was a part-time captain of the team. We finished the season with a mediocre record- I think it was 13 wins and 16 losses. What we did do was make the state tournament by taking second place in our district. And our district was loaded with strong teams. The seven other teams in our district were: Aztec, Socorro, Bernalillo, St. Pius, Academy, Los Lunas and Belen. We upset the powerhouse St. Pius to qualify for the state tournament. At the state tournament we reached my personal goal of winning one game. We beat Tucumcari in the first round of the tournament and finished 4th best in the state.

Basketball was a perfect fit for me. I was pretty much a loner and could practice on my own and I did. I set up a basketball goal in my backyard and practiced dribbling and shooting for hours at a time. I believed it was going to pay off eventually because I had a taste for winning and liked it. My next goal as a basketball player was to actually win the state tournament and be a state champion.

My senior year began with much anticipation and very high hopes. We started the year very confident with expectations of having a year even better than the last. So confident was I that at our first pep rally for the basketball squad I promised the student body that we would finish the season with thirty one wins and 0 losses and, bring home the state championship trophy. The season began mediocre at best.

We were eight and four by Christmas break and it seemed very dim for us to repeat last year's feat. We had lost one district game at home to Aztec and three road games in a double elimination tournament at the Roswell Invitational. Nevertheless I was determined not to let us lose another game during the rest of the season. Along the way we beat St. Pius, Academy and Bernalillo twice. In addition, we won the Gallup Invitational Tournament and also won the district tournament. We were going into the state tournament with a sixteen game winning streak. One of our opponents was Portales- one of the teams that had beaten us soundly at the Roswell Invitational. We however, were not the same team they had beaten earlier because we were experienced and prepared because we knew them and we knew about the pressures that came with the biggest tournament in the state. I believe they too were overconfident having beaten us earlier in the year.

Our starting five was all seniors. There was Jimmy, 6'-2" at center, Pete, 6'-1" at forward, Tommy, 6'-0' at the other forward, Michael, 5'-10" at the scoring guard position and me, 5'-9" at the point guard. Jimmy was known to be the most physical and aggressive center in our district if not the state. Pete was a blue chip player and was actually recruited by UNM and if not for his grades he might have played there. Tommy was the defensive specialist- if there was a super star on the opposing team it was his responsibility to shut him down. Michael was at the scoring position and many of the plays we ran were for his position. I was the point guard and it was my responsibility to bring the ball down court, break the press if there was one and set up the team to run set plays. It was up to me to choose which plays we ran and that was initiated by the first pass. That is, after the players were set in their proper positions I would determine what play was to be run by passing the ball to the right, left, center, inside or outside. We were a full court running and pressing team. We pressed every minute of the game causing the other teams to gradually lose their cool with the constant pressure.

As I remember we blew out Cobre in the first game of the state tournament (a game in which I played very poorly) and our next opponent was Portales. We had previously lost to Portales in the Roswell Invitational and I'm sure they were coming in overconfident having beaten us soundly in Roswell. We, however, were not the same team they had beaten earlier in the year. We were experienced and talented in every position and prepared. Our coach, Mr. Barber, told us that the only way to get revenge on West Las Vegas for having beaten us the year before in the state tournament is to get past Portales. We managed to squeak past them in a hard fought 68-60 victory and were headed for the AAA title game against West Las Vegas. Behind us was an eighteen game winning streak that we wanted to make nineteen. They had advanced to the title game by squeaking past Deming in a 71-69 squeaker. Deming was a team we had beaten early in the year at the Gallup Invitational Tournament.

West Las Vegas had had a fantastic year and was coming into the championship game with a 26-0 record. They were unbeaten! The only problem was- they hadn't played anyone during the year whereas we had played teams in Arizona and Colorado and teams in higher divisions than us. Before the season we had scrimmaged West Mesa, Highlands and Manzano and actually came out on top even though they were only scrimmages. During the season we had only lost to Clovis of all the teams in a division above us. The teams in a division above us that we had beaten were Farmington, Gallup, Rio Grande, Santa Fe and Roswell.

Coming into the tournament West Las Vegas was ranked No. 1 and we were ranked No. 2. We were the two best teams in our division and we met in the championship game. What follows is part of a close play-by-play account of that game that was written in the Grants Beacon March 16 of 1970 by Tommy Broadbent.

From the beginning of the game with West Las Vegas, it was obvious that two powerful machines were colliding head on. The first quarter was deadlocked until the closing minutes when the Grants, Pirates shot ahead to a six-point lead. Jimmy Harris put in three consecutive baskets from under the net early in the second to stretch the Pirates advantage to ten. The machine stayed on top of their ten-point cushion throughout the second period and part of the third. WLV's star John Allen was held to three points in the first half by Grants' tough defense and he committed three fouls.

In the second half the Dons began to move in on Grants with brilliant play by John Allen working with four fouls. Jimmy Harris who led both teams in scoring in the first had only made a field goal in the third quarter before he left the game with fouls. The Dons never got the lead but, in the fourth quarter, they pulled right up beside Grants on four occasions. It was 75-75 in the last minute to play and with a lay-up by Eddie Whorton, two free throws by Pete Gibson and two from the line by Walter Galles, the Pirates stayed on top of West Las Vegas whose final two points were put in by Allen.

The fouls that put Pete and Walter on the charity stripe in the last minute were the ones that sent Allen and Larry Baca, high scorer for the Dons, to the bench. Coach Don Barber stated that it was the mental conditioning that allowed Grants to stay cool under pressure and make the crucial shots. This was probably the main advantage the Red & Black had over West Las Vegas.

Friday morning, in the game that sent Grants to the finals, the Pirates romped over Portales 68-60 after being defeated by the Rams earlier in the season 65-45.

The machine didn't take the driver's seat for good until midway through the second period when they came from a two point deficit to score eight consecutive points and grab a six-point lead.

In the second half the Pirates were sparked on to a 10 point advantage with good play by Tommy Candell in probably his best performance of the year. Gibson, Harris and Candell fouled out late in the period. Walter Galles was the top scorer for Grants with 16 points followed by Pete Gibson with 14.

In the opening round of the State Tournament the Pirates had an easy though important win over Cobre Indians 75-55. Ten of the twelve machine members scored points with Gibson leading all scorers with 18 points.

Tournament Points: Gibson-53, Harris-36, Michael-36, Galles-34, E. Whorton-28, Candell-26.

Yes, we were the State Basketball Champions of the great state of New Mexico with an 81-77 win over West Las Vegas. Following the season Mr. Pete Gibson and I were selected by the team as co-captains. This honor I most greatly appreciated because I wanted it to be known that I was not only the point guard of the team but also the point man of the team. It was my personal goal to be a state champion and after having competed as a junior in the state tournament I knew it was possible. I was so certain we were going to win that I made a bet with Sam Jackson to that effect. The bet made on 10/29/69 stated that if we didn't win the state basketball tournament I would pay him $1.00 and if we did win he would pay me $1.00. Well, we won and he paid me and the agreement was signed as a witness by the Assistant Coach Luis Rivers. I still have that small document and I treasure it dearly as things following my high school senior year began to take a turn for the bad.

The year wasn't over yet, as I still had to compete in track. As far as track goes I ran the half-mile, high-jumped and occasionally ran a relay or two. We had a very good year in track and finishing second in the state meet. I qualified for the state meet by high-jumping 6'-0" during the season and finished 5th in the state meet with a jump of barely 6'-0". I finished the season and the year with a number or ribbons, letters and awards. The one I treasure most is the trophy for co-captain of the basketball team.

As far as the academics in high school go I barely finished with a 2.4 grade point average but was content with that GPA. As student council vice-president I learned that I won because of popularity and for no other reason. I certainly wasn't qualified to be student council vice-president as I didn't have the leadership qualities to lead anyone anywhere except if it was on a basketball court. I quickly learned that when I enrolled at a major university the following year.

IX

FROM HERO TO ZERO

Up to now everything in my life had happened in a small town at a smalltime scale with people I had known more or less much of my life. I was now a young adult and it was time to go out on my own. At eighteen years old I decided to go to college though I didn't have the least idea what to study or where to go to study. If not for my cousin Jimmy Harris influence and guidance I would have been completely lost. Since we had played the state tournament in Las Cruces at the Pan American Center and I was exposed to that school and campus it was easy to decide what school I wanted to go to. I chose New Mexico State University because my experiences there had all been so positive. What to study was the next problem. Jimmy suggested engineering technology and I didn't know any better so I enrolled in that discipline.

It happened to be a good match for me because I completely enjoyed that field of study. Fortunately for me it was the right major. If not for that I would have quickly flunked out and I don't know what would have happened to me then because at every other level I was a total failure.

At high school in Grants I was well adjusted, admired and appreciated but at NMSU it was a totally different story. The university alone was as big as the whole town I had just left and practically everyone was a complete stranger. Except for a few relatives I had no one to hang out with. I roomed for a time with an older sister and her husband then briefly with my cousin Jimmy. In other words- I was lost! No longer was I looked up to, I was nobody like everyone else. I was intimidated by the change and never able to adjust. I couldn't relate to other students or teachers. Friendships were difficult, if not impossible for me to make and I felt removed and distant from whatever situation I faced. In the 2½ years that I studied there I can't remember even one person I came to know personally. Although I made the grades and finished my studies on time and even had a respectable GPA there was a feeling of estrangement everywhere I went. I did everything with extreme caution- never allowing anyone to get close and eventually even lost old friendships from Grants. I was unable to trust anyone and old girlfriends that I had been somewhat intimate with became strangers. It got to the point where I couldn't connect anymore on a personal or social level with friends I had known and trusted for years. Social situations were impossible for me and I avoided them at all cost. The total extent of my social life involved basketball intramurals and going to the Aggies home basketball games and that was it.

Throughout my youth it never occurred to me that I might have a problem connecting with people. Being an athlete and very popular I always had plenty of friends male and female. The depth of those friendships always seemed comfortable, but looking back there never was any depth. All relationships I had with friends, male or female, were extremely shallow. The bond I had with my two closest friends throughout my adolescence and young adult years felt perfectly normal- anyway, as normal as friendships can be at that age. Once I got to college those two friendships began to erode and by the time I finished college they were complete strangers to me. For two friends to grow apart or for one to mature faster than another is perfectly normal but for them to become almost foreign to each other is abnormal, isn't it? That's the way all my friendships ended and for years and years I was never able to form new ones.

At NMSU I completed their two year program in Engineering Technology and got an Associate Degree in 2½ years then decided to study architecture. NMSU didn't have an architecture program so I transferred to the University of New Mexico which did. At UNM the situation was the same- socially I was unable to relate. I didn't even know enough students to join a basketball intramurals team. Two more years there studying architecture and I graduated with a Bachelor of Fine Arts with a major in architecture. All together I did 4½ years of university studies and can't remember one new individual I ever got to know personally. The best I can do as far as names go is to remember the names of two professors I studied under- Miss Carrey and Mr. Sulley.

X

EARLY ADULT YEARS

The result of not being able to form lasting relationships with female friends was the same throughout my early adult years. I had formed many friendships during my junior and high school years but all were at a very superficial level. This I didn't realize until many years later when one relationship after another ended and like I said before was unable to form new ones. There were girlfriends that I dated for months at a time but I always moved on from one girl to another without reason or closure from the one I left behind. For example, as a junior in high school there was Janice whom I dated for a time and went to the prom with and as a senior there was Sarah that I prommed with and dated for a while also but the same thing happened- I moved on without explanation.

And there were other girls that I dated briefly in between but always with the same result.

Following high school there was Audrey but this time things got a little more serious. We started seeing each other the summer after I graduated from high school and we saw each other off and on for about four or five years until I finally decided it was time to get engaged. So we began to make plans to get married. I thought she was the right girl for me but found out the hard way that she wasn't. One Christmas Holiday I was living and working in Denver and she was going to college in Santa Fe and we went to visit my old friend Tommy (my basketball teammate whom I had known since grade school) at his apartment in Albuquerque. After partying for hours with others we had been drinking beer and wine and even had a few puffs of pot, Audrey and I ended up in Tommy's bedroom. What actually happened that night I didn't recall until weeks later. I vaguely remembered the door to the bedroom opening and the light shining through and someone saying "Come with me, he's passed out." Little by little I was remembering and finally realized what she and Tommy had done to me. While at work one day it came to me that I wasn't dreaming that night, what I was thinking happened really did happen. I naturally broke off our engagement sometime later and to this day I don't know if she realizes why. She probably thinks that as I had a lot to drink and also smoked some pot that night I was too passed out to know the difference.

After being kicked in the teeth like that it would be hard for anyone to get back on the horse and ride again. And for me I didn't even want to look at another woman for some time to come. Though my personal and social life was in a sad situation I still had grand ambitions. I was still very young, had finished college and had a couple of degrees to show for it. I was anxious to face the future head on completely unaware of a haunting affliction that was going to rear its ugly head in due time.

XI

A NEW CHALLENGE

After graduating from college, although I didn't actually go through the graduation ceremony, I was off to find a job. In the middle of winter I was off to Denver in a red '68 Ford Maverick that smoked like a train and once a week I had to clean the spark plugs otherwise the carbon would cake on so thick it wouldn't start. On the way there I almost hit a deer on I-25 and was given a ticket for speeding. I must have been going downhill when the policeman caught me because that car could barely run. Anyway, I arrived safely in Denver and had made arrangements to stay with my older brother's friend who had recently moved there- John Darios and his family.

What I did to find a job is take the yellow pages of the phone book and literally go down the line alphabetically in the architectural section and visit practically every single office looking for a job. Needless to say, I went through the whole architecture section and came up empty. So, I started with the engineering section and did the same thing there. In a week and a half in Denver I must have visited at least a hundred offices with no luck. Finally I reached the S's in the yellow page phone book. There, in a small ad was listed Stone & Webster Engineering Corporation. I went to their office in Greenwood Plaza south of Denver and learned they were just opening a branch office. My timing couldn't have been more perfect because they were looking for draftsmen and that's exactly what I was qualified to do. Mr. Valens, a very tall man with a deep Russian accent, interviewed me and hired me on the spot. The pay was miserable- $5.70 per hour but I didn't care, I had found a job with a big company that offered me a future! Immediately I was told to report in mid-February to that office. So I packed my things and went home.

I learned that S & W was one of the largest engineering corporations in the world. They did mostly the design and construction management of power plants- fossil fuel, hydro-electric and nuclear. They also did roads, bridges, airports and many other projects. I was hired as a structural draftsman to work on the Rock Island Hydro-Electric Power Plant on the Columbus River in the state of Washington. Specifically, I was to draft the structural drawings for the powerhouse intake reinforcement stay-ring and intake liner embedment. Aside from that project I also worked on the North Valley Station Unit No. 1 of the Sierra Pacific Power Company in Winnemucca, Nevada. This was a fossil fuel power plant and my responsibility was to draft the framing plan of the boiler area at floor plan elevation 22'-0". I also drafted the railroad and road bridges and the abutments that were on the road to the site.

As far as I was concerned life was relatively good. There was not a lot of stress in being a draftsman and being single with no family responsibilities (partly because of the Tommy/Audrey betrayal). As it was, I worked for Stone & Webster for exactly two years and left on very good terms with the company. In fact there was a going away party for me when I left- so I at least had made a positive impression on the people I worked with. Towards the end of my time with S & W I began to get a little paranoid and suspicious about people in general. After all, two of the people I knew and trusted best had betrayed me a few months earlier. Even though others that I worked with were able to connect with me, I was unable to form any lasting or permanent relationships male or female. I left Denver for what I thought would lead to bigger and better opportunities elsewhere. Even while there I remember only going out to a night club once in two years to see Ray Charles. I had become a shut-in at the ripe old age of 24 never going out for fear that someone was going to 'get me.'

XII

A NEW DIRECTION

I was off to the San Francisco Bay Area to meet up with a fellow engineer (Hassam Abdul) that I had worked with at Stone & Webster. He left to go work with the Bechtel Corporation because they offered him more responsibility and better pay. That too was my hope- to land a job with Bechtel. That task, however, was much more difficult than I thought. I couldn't even get my foot in the door. So, I went looking for a job as I had before by going through the yellow pages alphabetically. This time I had two years of experience behind me and it proved to be an enormous asset. After a couple of weeks of searching I landed a job with a small architectural/engineering firm- Design and Engineering Systems. They did mostly the architectural and structural design and construction management of industrial office parks.

The firm's office was in Redwood City and I rented an apartment in Foster City- a 20 minute drive down Highway 101. My one bedroom apartment was on the second floor with a patio and a view out to the swimming pool. At a local furniture store I bought a country style living room set and also some bedroom furniture but there was a delay in the delivery so for the first couple of weeks I slept on the floor. With some help from my friend Hassam I found my way around the Bay Area and made the adjustment to the very fast pace of life. He introduced me to Greg Dababo whom at the time was working for The Bechtel Corporation and we became good friends.

Again, I was hired to be a structural draftsman with hopes of someday soon of being given the opportunity to do some architectural design. That, however, never happened there because I was working with young architects from Berkeley and Harvard. What I didn't know about this place of employment was that it was a sweatshop. For months I was sometimes working more than 70 hours a week at a salary of about $310 a week including overtime. This firm was extremely busy when I was hired and when things slowed down they simply laid me off just as quick. I didn't bother filing for unemployment because I was doing part-time drafting for David Kelley/Architect and had him as a backup source of income. When things picked up again DES called and asked me to come back but I told them no, of course, because there was too much work out there to work for a company like that again.

What the circumstances were and how I ended up working for

another architect in Oakland I don't know but there I was with Keith Archer/Architect for a while. Things had just begun to unravel for me. There are months at this time in my life which I look back now that were all a blur. The fast pace of the lifestyle I was living was taking its toll on me. The commute from Foster City to Oakland across the San Mateo Bridge and up Interstate 880 was well over an hour by car and I was making it every day in addition to working long hours. I don't know exactly how long I worked for Mr. Archer and I don't know if he let me go or if I quit. All I know for sure is that his office was in his home somewhere in Oakland on Zinn Street and that I briefly worked for him. There were times in the car when I found myself screaming out at the top of my lungs trying someway to relieve the stress that was bottled up inside me. I would get home at night so stressed out that I couldn't sleep so I'd go out and shoot baskets but the neighbors complained and put an end to that. I would go for a swim or take a jog around the marina but nothing helped- I couldn't sleep. Finally I went to a psychiatrist and he hypnotized me and did help me sleep one night but at more than one dollar a minute that was way beyond my means.

To make things worse on myself, my friend Greg told me that Bechtel was hiring. He also told me exactly whom to send my resume to. So I did- I sent it to Mr. Rob Runnels and within a few days I had a call from his office to set up a job interview. I took some of my freelance architectural renderings and he was impressed. The following 5 pages are some of the drawings I showed him at the interview. They are hand drawn renderings of high-rise buildings as I had a fascination with tall buildings at the time.

DRAWING 1

DRAWING 2

DRAWING 3

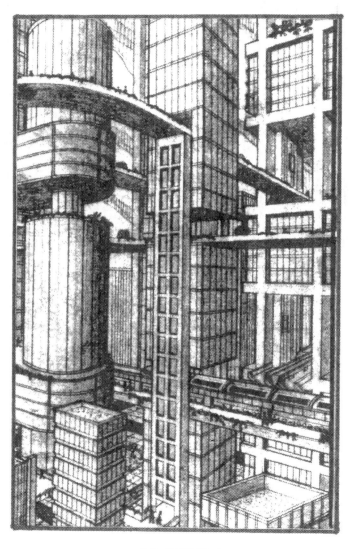

DRAWING 4

DRAWING 5

After Mr. Runnels saw these and other drawings he hired me on the spot. These renderings and a few others had been drawn during many sleepless nights. Of course, I brought with me drawings from my Stone & Webster days as well as other drawings from other offices where I had worked in the Bay Area. Bechtel Corporation at that time occupied several high-rise buildings in downtown San Francisco and employed about nine thousand people. They worked on the design of some of the world's largest construction projects-buildings, bridges, airports, power plants or whatever other projects anyone who has the finances to build Bechtel would design and build.

Personally, the short time I was there, I mainly worked on the Dubai International Airport. Specifically, I worked on the design for the catering facility for that airport and made many detail drawings for airport hangars and gas stations. I also, very briefly, worked on the Waste Isolation Pilot Plant in Carlsbad, New Mexico. In the building where I worked I started on the 9th floor and before I left was on the 32nd floor with a great view of the San Francisco Bay. My departure from the Bay Area was done in a mode of desperation as my thinking had become extremely senseless.

XIII

ESCAPE FROM SAN FRANCISCO

While working for Bechtel the future seemed very good- just as at Stone & Webster, but the pressure of commuting early in the morning and returning late in the evening after a full day's work was too much for me to handle. The normal everyday stress of the job, typical for millions of others, was too much for me. On top of that, I was beginning to study for the architectural license in the state of California. Sleepless nights and poor eating habits didn't help the situation. The paranoia and suspicions I had toward fellow workers heightened. When overhearing a conversation at a distance between others, it somehow got in my head that they were talking about me and that they knew me and plotting to harm me. In other words, I was thinking that they were out to 'get me.' My thinking was irrational but it seemed so real. I couldn't explain what I was experiencing to anyone because my suspicions included everyone. There was no one I could talk to. It got to the point that I missed work on Fridays- instead I went in on Saturdays when I could work alone one day. That only worked for a couple of months- the paranoia was getting worse. Everywhere I went it was the same. I just couldn't trust anyone. Even at my apartment, when there were people outside talking and I couldn't make out what they were saying I thought they were talking about me. Finally, after only one year with Bechtel and almost three years in the San Francisco Bay Area I had to leave.

While working at Bechtel I had made a few friends. I'm sure they wondered what happened to me because my departure was so abrupt. My 'escape' from San Francisco was done in desperation, thinking I was leaving all the paranoia and suspicions behind. It was a hopeless situation for me. With everyone trying to get me I was at one point crawling around on the carpet in my apartment like a baby. In complete despair I cried out at the top of my lungs "GOD HELP ME," and believe it or not at that very moment the phone rang. It was an old acquaintance, Esmeralda. She was a very, very religious young lady that on many occasions had tried to get me to read the bible. I tried to tell her what was happening and she advised me to come home. We talked for a while and she calmed me down and got me thinking rationally long enough to pack my things and leave. It turned out she had briefly experienced the same kind of paranoia and also had a sense of what was really happening to me. She told me I was being persecuted and my thinking was so unsound I believed her.

On the way out I took apart my furniture and was in the process of throwing everything away into the dumpster. The janitor came by and asked me what I was doing and I asked him if he could use a set of living room and bedroom furniture and he of course jumped on it. What couldn't fit into my little blue Toyota Celica I tossed into the dumpster. My car was loaded with clothes, books, a TV, a guitar and a lot of other things. I got on the San Mateo Bridge thinking the police wouldn't know me or be looking for me on the east side of the Bay. No one, of course, was looking for me but in my mind I was being followed everywhere I went. I even left at night thinking I was sneaking out so no one would know. What I couldn't get out of my head was that no one knew me and no one cared what I did. If I saw a police car I deliberately made a U-turn, or made other efforts to avoid them thinking they were out looking for me. Nevertheless, I took Highway 880 south to Highway 101 towards Los Angeles to my Aunt Soriada's house.

On the freeway I was deliberately trying, for some stupid suicidal reason, to get in to an accident. At one point I squeezed between two eighteen wheelers that were driving very close and very fast hoping they would run me over. All night long I drove like a madman headed for Los Angeles. While driving through San Luis Obispo I heard sirens blasting in the opposite direction. My first thought was they are looking for me. Fearing it was the police who had been waiting and were now coming for me I took the nearest exit and hid somewhere in a darkened neighborhood. I stayed there until it was quiet, and then threw the rest of my stuff into the nearest dumpster I could find. A car full of partying teenagers stopped and asked what I was doing. I told them I was throwing away things I didn't want and if they wanted them they could have them. I actually emptied my car. The clothes, books, guitar and everything else in the car I tossed. Then I rested a while and eventually got back on the road and headed for L.A.

When I got to Los Angeles I was thinking that if the police want me they can have me. So I drove straight into the police station and parked inside the underground parking facility. I went and sat on the steps of the police station expecting to be hauled away at any minute. I waited and waited but nothing happened. I just sat there on the steps of the City Hall like an idiot in the middle of the night. Finally, I walked to the nearest payphone in the nearest bar and called my aunt to come pick me up. It just happened that she lived less than fifteen minutes from the police station so my uncle picked me up quickly. I wanted to abandon my car where I parked it but my uncle wouldn't let me so we went for the car and I followed him home. Even so, I was afraid once the police saw my car they would know where I was and they'd come get me.

Still unable to sleep, and in L.A. it was worse there because of the helicopters flying overhead all night. At one point they were so loud that it seemed as if they were directly overhead and I of course thought they were looking for me. Not only could I not sleep but I also didn't let my aunt and uncle sleep. I woke them up and kept telling them, "There they are, they're looking for me. They're coming to get me." My aunt and uncle couldn't understand why I was saying that because they heard the helicopters every night. They finally went to sleep and told me to do the same but not until after I had sold them my car. I was so desperate to dump my car that I convinced them to buy it and they bought it at a dirt cheap price. It was only a year old, it had less than 11,000 miles and I bought it for $7,700 and sold it for around $2,000. What happened to that money I don't have the slightest clue because when I got home I was completely broke. All I had with me was the clothes on my back and a box of drafting tools.

The next day my aunt called my parents and told them what was happening with me. My parents came a couple days later and visited for a few days then we flew home to Albuquerque together. What was happening to me on the way to the airport was strange, new, and to say the least, very unfamiliar. While in the backseat of the car what I was experiencing was peculiar. As we drove by every person I saw I thought was reacting to me. Every movement and every little gesture that every person made in my twisted mind was a reaction to me. My thinking was completely crazy. I was paranoid in every sense of the word but I didn't know this. To me, everything was really happening to me. I was literally the center of the world- that is, everyone knew me, and I was a giant target for everyone. I know this sounds ridiculous, but when the mind is completely out of control and thinking unreasonably it seems as if everything (I mean everything) is happening to me, for me, at me, and because of me.

XIV

HOME AGAIN

The next thing I can remember is being where I belonged-in a psychiatric ward in Albuquerque in a straightjacket with one foot tied to a bed. How I got there I can only vaguely recall. My uncle Frank, my cousin Manuel, my younger brother and my father physically put me into a car and forcibly took me to the hospital. While on the way to the hospital I remember screaming out something about the "Japanese are attacking and you don't even know!" What the hell that meant I'll never know. I was there for a couple of weeks (I think) and was given medication to last for a couple of months. The good doctor (Dr. Levi) diagnosed me as a paranoid schizophrenic and prescribed Haldol for the schizophrenia and Cogentin for the side effects.

After my thinking was straight again and my behavior

was back to normal I was released to my parent's custody and was sent home. Miraculously, a few weeks later UPS delivered all the 'stuff' I had dumped at San Luis Obispo to my parent's house. How this came about I'm not quite sure. With a few months of rest, good food and loving attention I felt well enough to go out and look for a job. There were several places I applied and was offered work at two of the largest Engineering Corporations in the Southwest-Bohannon Huston Engineering and Herkenhoff Engineering Corporation. My cousin Porter worked at BH and he was the brother of Manuel who had months earlier helped put me in a mental ward. So, I took the job with Herkenhoff as a structural, civil and architectural draftsman. Once again I started at a low salary but I was happy to take the job because it meant that I was able to work again.

Things at Herkenhoff went along just fine for a couple of years. I worked there doing what I was told and almost never caused any problems. For the most part, I settled in and was secure as a draftsman working on a great number of projects though I can't recall any. The projects I worked on were usually small compared to jobs I had worked on at S & W and Bechtel.

My paranoia and suspicions did surface within a few months but I was satisfied to believe it was something normal and dealt with it as such. I went to work every day and led my daily life as normally as I possibly could. All the while I couldn't shake the paranoia and was still unable to trust or let anyone get close to me physically, emotionally, or socially. I look back now at this time in my life, and at Herkenhoff, and realize that most people that knew me then were thinking I was a little strange. My behavior was so peculiar I can understand why. For example, if an attractive girl showed an interest in me I would, for no reason at all completely put her off. If there was a company gathering I made it a point not to go or if I did go my behavior socially, at least on one occasion, was embarrassing. I remember playing on the company softball team for a while but can't recall what caused me to leave the team. Generally, I had very little to do with the people I worked with and they, I'm sure, thought I was more than a little weird. There was one occasion when I was hospitalized while working there that I can only vaguely remember. I don't know why or for what reason I was put in the hospital.

I worked with Herkenhoff well over two years and one day was asked by my boss to move on. I wasn't fired, I think, because he told me exactly where to go to get another job. He even told me who to talk to at the other office and I was quickly hired at the other place. It's as if he had made prior arrangements with the other office to have me hired. They probably didn't want to pay unemployment. I was let go on a Thursday at Herkenhoff Engineering and on the following Monday I was working at Crego Block Company.

XV

DESPERATE TIMES

Working at Crego Block Company was enjoyable. My duty there simply was to draft precast concrete roof and/or floor panels. These panels were 4ft. wide and either 8" or 12" thick and were cut to whatever length was called for. The 12" thick ones could span as much as 45ft. and the 8" ones could span as much as 30ft. I worked in an office practically alone because I was the only draftsman. The structural engineer had an office next to mine and he was responsible for checking my drawings. He was an alcoholic and many of my drawings went unchecked. That meant there were mistakes that got by that I was in the end blamed for. The panels for one small project in Farmington, New Mexico were cut too long and this was not discovered until they were shipped to the site. This meant the ruin of a small contractor and also the beginning of the end of my time at Crego. My time there lasted only about a year, but before I left, there was my second hospitalization.

My paranoid thinking was still haunting me. I was convinced the boss himself and the people I worked with were after me. There was no way for me to maintain a working relationship with the other workers at this place because I couldn't trust them. It was my belief that someone was sabotaging my drawings, though I never brought this up because I had no proof. My attitude toward others was contentious because of my false suspicions. It got to be very, very stressful for me. So much so, that I went to my apartment one evening and attempted suicide.

I thought about what direction my life was taking and decided that it wasn't worth living. I talked myself into believing that I was worthless to the world and more importantly, to myself. I took my pocketknife, (the same pocketknife my father had infamously used on others) lay down on the couch, and started to cut my wrist but the damn knife was so dull I couldn't cut anything. I sharpened it as best I could then I began cutting my left wrist. It was late, I was tired and I was only able to cut about a 1" gash on my wrist. I held my hand down, fell asleep on the couch and was hoping I would bleed to death while in my sleep. I woke up a few hours later and all I had done was ruin a perfect purple windbreaker with blood stains that I set on the floor so as not to stain the carpet.

Then, when I awoke I was very much still alive, and as I lay on the couch I noticed a long TV cable cord coming out of the wall. So I cut a piece six feet long and stupidly tried to hang myself with it. I tested the cord and it was strong enough to hold my weight. I put a plastic bag around my head and a chair in the closet. Then I tied the cord around the closet cross bar, got on my knees on the chair in the closet and wrapped the cord around my neck, tied my hands behind my back with a belt, then kicked the chair out from under me with my knees. I hung for a very short time until the cord snapped then I lay there groping on the floor for twenty minutes, maybe more. My thinking was that if I didn't hang myself to death I would suffocate. Not so, I managed to untie myself and got up frustrated to be alive again but relieved not to be sucking on plastic. All I got for this was a temporary scar around my neck.

In the same apartment and on the same night I wasn't finished killing myself. I went to a 24 hour pharmacy and bought two bottles of Extra Strength Excedrin. On the way home I bought a large coke with ice, dissolved the two boxes of pills in the coke and began to drink. I drank and drank till I almost finished my concoction but it was already very early in the morning and my father came knocking at the door. He found me half asleep/half drugged and the evidence of my stupidity all over the apartment floor.

Again I was hospitalized. This time I was forced to drink a twelve ounce glass of what tasted like carbon at the hospital to vomit up all the Excedrin I had consumed- something that I will never forget. Again, I was diagnosed as a paranoid schizophrenic, given a prescription for a few weeks supply of anti-psychotics and sent home. I don't have the slightest recollection what medication I was given. In my mental state there was no way I could hold down any kind of job. Especially considering the fact that I was in serious denial and wouldn't admit, (Probably because I actually didn't know) that I was extremely ill.

Nevertheless, I went back to work at Crego and after all that the boss hounded me daily. He wanted me out of that office and in a short time achieved his objective. Finally, I didn't show up for work a couple of days without calling. When I returned there was another draftsman in my desk using all my drafting tools. I hadn't shown up because this time the boss really was out to get me and I needed a way out of the stress and the pressure. He told me I was just being delusional, on top of being paranoid and suspicious. Which was all true but I had no idea just how sick I actually was. In reality, I did have difficulty relating to people, I couldn't think straight, couldn't hold down an easy job, and didn't know what to do next.

XVI

INTO THE MILITARY

After having lost the Crego job I wondered what could I do and the only thing I could think of was to find another job. So I went looking for another one, and again to my surprise, found one. It was a drafting job like before, but once again, I was in no condition to hold down any kind of job. Why I thought I could hold on to this one I have no idea. The same thing happened here as at all other places- I was unable to think straight. Unlike at Stone & Webster where I could perform difficult tasks and perform them well I was now unable to draw even a simple floor plan. I only lasted at this office for the six months trial period then I was given two week's pay and told good-bye. I can't even remember the name of the company or any of the people I worked with for the six months I was there.

I eventually lost my apartment and moved in with my parents while I tried to regroup and decide what to do next. Out of work for nearly six months and living off my parents I had to do something, so next I did the only thing I could think of- try to join the military. The Army seemed like the perfect solution to my problem. I went to the local recruiting office and filled out the questionnaire as best I could and it obviously was good enough to get me in the army.

I was sent to Basic Training in Fort Jackson, South Carolina as an Administrative Specialist. Basic was not an easy chore because I went in way out of shape at 208 pounds. I learned, much to my surprise, that I was not the only thirty plus year old trainee. There were two other soldiers slightly older than me and I presume they were also in a down and out situation like me. I got to be good friends with one- David Dey, he was from San Antonio and had two children. He had lost his job as an accountant and was unable to find another so he joined the military. I never got to know the other 'senior' in our battalion.

During Basic I was physically able to complete all exercises except the twenty eight kilometer march which proved to be too much for me. At the twenty two km mark I started to drop off pace and at the twenty four km mark I was put into the back of a truck and taken to where we were going. In spite of this, I was competing with 18, 19 and 20 year old soldiers and finished somewhere near the top of the class. I qualified expert with the rifle. At the end of Basic I weighed 183 pounds. The other two soldiers my age were allowed to slide on just about everything except meals.

Next was Advanced Individual Training (AIT) and it proved to be fun, fun, fun. There were girls in the classes- lots of girls, pretty ones and ugly ones- very, very ugly ones. While in AIT I had at least two proposals of marriage. I didn't say no to either, I just suggested that we get to know each other first. We never did, of course, because they went their way and I went mine- to Germany.

In Germany I was stationed at a very small detachment near the North Sea called, Hohenkirchen. Our mission there was to guard two underground nuclear silos that I never saw. As administrative specialist I was always stuck in the office typing up paper work for the First Sergeant, the Commanding Officer or the Executive Officer. I typed up letter after letter after letter for them and did my very best without worrying what others were thinking. I co-operated with the mission to the extent of my responsibilities and no further. I woke up at 4:30 A.M. every morning to make it to Physical Training (PT) at 5:30 A.M. and was at work by 7:30 A.M. I had a normal working schedule from 7:30 A.M. to 5:00 P.M. and was at work every day and don't remember missing a single day. I was home by 6:30 P.M. ate dinner, watched some television then fell asleep by 9:00 P.M. and was ready and well rested for the next day. In other words I did the very best to be the best soldier I could possibly be as long as I was physically and mentally able.

I had been there about six months when my life began to spiral out of control- again. The paranoia, the delusions, the suspicions and the freight train I was hauling behind me started to run me over. It all began when I was placed on a twenty four hour shift and I began to lose sleep. Not only was I losing sleep but I was imagining other soldiers plotting things against me. My responsibilities were much more than just typing letters for the bosses. It meant staying up day and night observing and responding to correspondence between other detachments with the same mission. This mission seemed simple enough and it was, for any soldier with a normal thought pattern but for me it was stress at an unmanageable level. At one point, I attempted to check out my M16, but fortunately they didn't let me. While in my apartment one sleepless night I wrote the following poem. This poem is about suicide and how when thoughts of suicide come they take over a person's being to leave one in complete despair and confusion. In this instance I was in a foxhole with an M16 at a firing range when the enemy I was fighting within me tried to overpower me and make me shoot myself.

THE FOXHOLE

My foxhole gave me a clear and almost perfect view of ambitions gone in disarray, of dreams taken in silence by a cruel and desperate thief.

Completely unaware was I of that rogue that knew me well. Scope me out did he. Then- with tact, with patience, with convenience did he attack.

My sensibilities, my soul, my being was his aim. To drive me from my self was his goal. With vigilance and with precision he sought to leave me stranded in confusion.

What was I to do? When that unwanted foreigner comes he comes to claim you for his own. How indeed can one uncloak his well-conceived disguise?

Yes, there in that quaint and private little foxhole I was ready to cooperate completely with my foe. To take me, time and time again he would threaten.

Don't you see, I am the more clever, I am in control, I am the one who will not yield, he would say to me. To drop and cover me up was his intent.

To confound my every thought, my every emotion, my every step was his ambition. Forget your bearings, he would utter in my brain, I will control this being.

Relate yourself to no one. Others have no clue what we're about. You dream to be an architect do you? A scholar on the subject you think.

You want to be a historian of some sort- how senseless you are. Between here and there you cannot even walk the line. Why peruse yourself away.

Every window will be broken, every door sealed, I will be there to confiscate your every move. In time you will be mine- yes, in time you will be mine.

Go ahead- place that M16 below your chin. Qualify you expert or qualify oblivion. Stun the cadre, show them how irrelevant you and they are.

Shatter your thoughts all over their well-pressed cammies. Drop an everlasting memory all over their highly polished boots. Color the walls.

Color the ceiling, color the floor, color them all in dreams and aspirations, along with those nightmares and fantasies you haul.

As I said, stress was unimaginable and unmanageable for

me and I began plotting suicide. It never went beyond just thoughts. On one occasion late at night I got in my car and tied myself to the seat with a rope thinking I'd drive myself off the Wilmshaven dock into the water and drown. I cowered and it didn't happen though with the same rope I went home and down the street to a wooded area I tossed it around a tree branch- but again I couldn't do it. On that same night I tried to get into a high rise apartment building to jump off but the doorman wouldn't let me in. Any person with suicidal thoughts is obviously ill. I was still unwilling to admit that I had a mental condition that had to be remedied one way or another. After all, the last thing a person wants to admit is having a mental illness- and I was no different.

XVII

EUROPEAN VACATION

In an effort to relieve the stress I was experiencing it occurred to me that a vacation might help. Where better to vacation than in Europe? Vacations are generally taken to relieve stress, aren't they? Well, that was my intent. With me in Germany were my three young nephews and their mother- the widow of my older brother who had committed suicide about ten years earlier. At the time she and I had a loving relationship. The five of us climbed into my green, ten year old BMW and started to tour Europe. We planned on our final destination to be Madrid, Spain.

We went west from West Germany to Holland then southwest to Belgium and further south to Paris, France. I don't remember clearly if we spent the first night on the road in Amsterdam or Brussels but I do remember the next two nights we stayed in Paris. We rented a couple of rooms at the Phenix Hotel near the Arc de Triomphe in downtown Paris. That I recall clearly because a movie was being shot on the Champs Elysee near the Arc and the streets were blocked off. So unaware was I of what was happening (or I didn't care) that I jumped the barrier to cross the street and almost got arrested. (By the way, I think it was a James Bond movie) The second night we left the boys at the hotel and went to the Moulin Rouge. It seemed like the vacation was going to do what I had intended- relieve the stress.

The next day we were on the road again for another straight eight or nine hours and I learned very quickly that my intentions to eliminate stress were very, very wrong. With three pre-teen boys in the back seat and a woman in the front seat telling me exactly where we were and where we were going every minute I was only making my condition worse- much worse. Nevertheless, we continued with our plans to drive on into Spain. I recall driving through France for hours and hours and listening to the radio in French but I could swear I could hear my name being spoken. The only thing I could make out was my name over and over and over again. This of course was because I was delusional. I wasn't hearing my name it was just in my mind that I was.

At one point I was so frustrated that I ripped the map from Mary's hand, stopped at a garbage bin and threw it away. From there on we were following the wind. How we got around in Paris without a map I'll never know. But we got in and out and on our way towards Spain without a problem. We drove all through France and all I knew is we were headed south and eventually crossed the Pyrenees and were well into Spain. In Spain I could understand the radio station disc jockeys and it seemed to me as if all they were talking about was me. It seemed as if they knew every move I was making and that they were following my every move. Every time we stopped for gasoline I could swear all those people knew who I was and were trying to control my every thought.

Needless to say, we didn't make it to our final destination- Madrid. I recall seeing a sign one hundred fifty kilometers to Madrid but I had enough. I took a detour to Zaragoza, Spain. It just so happened we were in the State of Zaragoza and I also saw a sign that said U.S. Air Force Base seventy kilometers. So, we went to the air base and checked in for a couple days of much needed rest. I, however, was the only one needing rest- they were having a blast. Once again the freight train had caught up with me and was about to run me over if I didn't do something soon. I rested and dealt with the situation as best I could. Fighting off the paranoia and voices telling me I was wasting my time. That I was no good, that I was worthless but I couldn't give in to the voices and paranoia I was in the middle of Spain and was responsible for getting my family safely back to Germany.

On the way back to Germany Mary wanted to go to Barcelona so we went east and stopped there for a few hours. I remember visiting the Sagrada Familia Cathedral by Antonio Gaudi. It is an architectural masterpiece that I had studied in college and also wanted to see. We had lunch across the street from it on the sidewalk. After that we headed straight back to Germany making a stop in Paris once again for a couple more days of rest before making the final few hundred kilometers home.

I returned to Germany no more rested than before. In fact I

was worse. I was already unable to sleep and think rationally when a phone call from back home came that my father had had an aneurysm and was critically ill. I immediately drove with Carl, the eldest of my three nephews, to Munich to catch a flight to Albuquerque. We flew home via Chicago and when we arrived my father was in a coma at the VA Hospital. We were home for about a week and when it seemed like he was improving and that he might recover we returned to Germany.

We were back in Germany only a few days when one of my sisters called to inform me that my father had died. Once again I drove with my nephew Nick (the middle nephew) to Munich for a flight to Albuquerque. This time, on the way to Munich suicidal thoughts started creeping in again and at night with car lights flashing by on a two-way highway construction zone, I had it in my mind to sway the car ever so slightly to the left. Fortunately, I didn't do it. Nick and I arrived in Albuquerque safe and sound. Well, Nick was safe, but I was not sound by any means.

While in Albuquerque I somehow, somewhere ran into my cousin Jimmy. We had played basketball together in high school and he had mentored me while I was in college at NMSU. We hadn't seen each other for many years and decided to take a weekend drive up to his cabin in the mountains above Pecos, New Mexico. I took my father's high powered rifle with me thinking we might do some shooting while up there. What I was really thinking was to do the same thing my older brother had done. "He did it," I thought, "It can't be that difficult to blow my brains out in the middle of the night." All night long up in the loft I held the rifle under my chin with my finger on the trigger.

I cowered, again. Sleepless, tired and hungry that morning I didn't mention a word to my cousin or anyone else what I had planned on doing that night. We had breakfast and drove back down that morning.

I was so distraught, paranoid and confused that I didn't even make it to my own father's funeral. Not only did I not make it to his funeral, I didn't immediately make it back to Germany. No, no I didn't go AWOL this time because a few days after the funeral we caught a flight back to Germany via Dallas, but that's as far as we got because I thought I heard my name again and again over the intercom system at the airport. I swear that I heard the male voice on the intercom saying, "There he goes, look at that idiot, don't let him get away, there he goes… I'm talking to you- yes you, you stupid idiot, you won't get away this time, I know you… etc." I quickly made a U-turn at the Dallas airport with my young nephew in hand and we headed back to Albuquerque. We stayed there for another three or four more weeks until I thought it was 'safe' to return to Germany. Eventually we made it back safely.

XVIII

REALITY SINKS IN

I was back on duty and when my 24-hour shift came around I did my very best to complete it successfully. At least I know I tried- half an hour before my shift was to end I actually left my post. After being cramped up in that tiny closet with all that communications equipment for twenty three and a half long hours the torrential voices in my head got to me and I couldn't take it anymore so I just walked out. Fortunately, my friend Sgt. Harold was driving in to come on duty saw me walking down the street and yelled out at me, "What the hell are you doing? Where the hell you going? Get your ass back here!" I didn't get written up or even reprimanded for that incident because only Sgt. Harold and a couple other soldiers knew what I had done.

On the way home I literally fell asleep behind the wheel,

drove my car straight into a steel garage door and briefly knocked myself out as well as knock out a few teeth on the steering wheel. Fortunately, it was a thick steel garage door because there were two men welding inside. When my commanding officer found out about this he grounded me to the barracks day and night. He thought I was driving under the influence and I couldn't convince him otherwise. On top of that I tried to explain to him what was happening to me but he wouldn't even listen much less try to understand. I explained my situation to my supervising sergeant (Sergeant Warren) and she told me she would make an appointment for me at the hospital in Bremerhaven. When I went to the appointment she had supposedly made for me there was no record of a call from her at the hospital. (Now, as I look back on that time in Germany I think all my supervisors were thinking I was just looking for a way to get out of the military.)

It was Mary who later drove me to the hospital and I went in without an appointment. I explained to a nurse what was happening to me and she quickly made arrangements for me to see a doctor. The psychiatrist there immediately admitted and medicated me. He made arrangements for me to be further evaluated in Mannheim and was flown there the next day by helicopter. I was briefly hospitalized there in a mental ward though I have no idea how long I was there. From there I was medically evacuated to the states. I recall being given a couple of sandwiches with a few pills in a cargo plane and the next thing I knew I was in a Bethesda, Maryland hospital waiting to be sent to the Medical Evaluation Board at Sheppard Air Force Base in Wichita Falls, Texas.

I was at Sheppard for a couple of months, I think, and my diagnosis was as follows: "schizoaffective disorder; chronic, with recent exacerbation; severe, currently in remission on medication." I now had no doubts about my mental health. I was schizophrenic and it was a chronic condition. What the Army did was to give me a few months of medication, release me from the hospital and discharge me with a good behavior medal.

The Army said I should, "receive psychiatric follow-up at a clinic of his choice." Luckily I located a clinic near my mother's home in Albuquerque and did receive some follow-up treatment. However, I was not going to let this mental illness get the best of me and went out looking for a job. Shortly, after my discharge an engineering company hired me as a structural draftsman. I didn't even last two weeks. The voices I heard in my head and outside my head just wouldn't let me concentrate on even the simplest of tasks. This time the voices I heard in my brain were so distinct and powerful I thought the co-workers directly behind me were deliberately goading me. I could swear I heard someone say, "So you're Jesus Christ, huh? Imagine that, the Prince of Peace working with me. Is your father coming for you?" For every eight hours I was there I was hearing voices constantly making references to me that I was Jesus Christ that I was the Son of God that I could make miracles happen. In a couple of weeks it got to where I couldn't take anymore so I walked out and never went back.

I was just unable to work and at my oldest sister's suggestion I applied for Social Security Disability. I went to the Social Security office and asked for the forms to apply, and did so on my own. I filled out the forms as best I could but was quickly denied. My sister suggested I go to the local Legal Aid and they helped me through the process. The second appeal was also denied. The paralegal- Sally, who was assigned to my case, reviewed my medical history and told me that on the third appeal I'll have to go before a judge and he will make a determination and it will be approved. How could they deny me with the medical track record I had? The judge, on the third appeal, approved my request for disability. I was getting paid $610 a month.

With a steady source of income, necessary medication and regular psychiatric treatment all was well for the next few years. I now had some stability in my life and was even able to form a lasting friendship with a very special person I met. A few years in the past, when I was able, I had enjoyed playing the guitar and had recently picked it up again and even tried my hand at writing songs. That is how I met my friend, Antonio. He was the coordinator of a club called The Musicians and Song Writers of New Mexico. I went to check this place out because I wanted somehow to market my songs and thought this would be a perfect avenue. Antonio was an accomplished guitar player and songwriter himself. We hit it off from the start. I was schizophrenic and he was blind so we both understood what it was like living with a disability.

Antonio became an inspiration to me because he was able to live a perfectly normal life despite his disability. He had a wife and two young sons that he was able to support on his disability income. He, however, was always looking for a way to get out from under the restrictions Social Security imposed on him and in time he did. He went to school, studied to become a massage therapist and currently has been running his own successful business for years without the need of Social Security Disability.

Now that I look back at those first few years when I got to know Antonio I think he all the while had the better situation. Yes, he is virtually all blind- but his mind was able to function at one hundred per cent, whereas mine, without medication, is 'all screwed up.' He had a memory that could recall a voice he had met from years before. He could remember directions to a certain address he had been to years before. In other words, he was, and continues to be, a person with remarkable abilities able to overcome his obvious disability without much of a problem. Don't misunderstand me- I am perfectly aware that his blindness is a major handicap, but he makes it look easy to be blind. I often wanted to change places with him because life for him was worth the effort. For me, as you have read, life at times was very suicidal. Because I met this man, life for me too has become not only worth the effort but has taken me beyond anywhere I ever dreamed of going. Like I said, I was, and still am inspired by this man (although we do have our differences and I strongly do not agree with some of his political views) I am as determined to overcome my handicap as he is to live life as if there are no handicaps. Like they say, a mind can be a terrible thing to waste and I intend to make the very most of this one.

XIX

A SCHIZOPHRENIC EPISODE

With some stability in my life, along with my mother, we decided to move to a nicer neighborhood. And we did, but because of the move I had to find another source of treatment and medication. At the local county clinic I found what I needed. There was a problem with my medications though. Some medications were more effective than others. Depending on which doctor I saw determined the medication I was on. As doctors move on, retire, or experiment with medications so I was put on several different medication. For a time I was on Haldol but it had side effects that I couldn't deal with. Then I was on Prolixin but the doctor who prescribed it left his practice. I was also on Thioridizine and it served me well for a few years but the doctor that prescribed it retired. Following Thioridizine I was put on a low dose of Abilify, then Zyprexa. Between the time I was on Thioridizine and Zyprexa I was also briefly on Seroquel and Risperdal. The time from Haldol to Zyprexa involved a number of years but all that time I had a steady supply of medication and had few psychiatric problems.

I was on Zyprexa for approximately four years until my psychiatrist decided to leave his practice. He left at about the same time it became public that Zyprexa had a side- affect that was chronic. It was giving people all over the country diabetes and I was included. I learned about this when I saw an ad on television that Zyprexa had many side-affects and one of them was diabetes. But even after my doctor had stopped prescribing it to me he had given me many, many samples and I was still taking it months afterwards. Two and a half years after I started taking Zyprexa I was diagnosed with diabetes. Aware of the serious medical problems associated with diabetes, I was already fearful about it and was always cautious and deliberate about taking my medication for diabetes and followed a strict diabetes diet. Believing that the bad effects were worse than its anti-psychotic benefits, I immediately stopped taking Zyprexa.

As I mentioned earlier I had no problems while on medications, however, my nearly ten year streak without a schizophrenic episode came to an end. My psychiatrist had informed me that he was going to semi-retire and I would have to find another psychiatrist to treat my schizophrenia.

After many phone calls I was finally able to find another psychiatrist to treat me and made arrangements for a first appointment. He prescribed a very low dose of Abilify (Aripriprazole) but for whatever reason it did not work for me and I soon began experiencing another schizophrenic episode. I began feeling paranoid, worthless, guilty and believing people were out to get me. Despite the fact that I actually knew that these were some of the symptoms of schizophrenia I had no control over them and gradually these feelings began to overwhelm me. For days or weeks, I don't know which, I was feeling like this. I lay in my bedroom thinking that at any time someone was going to come in and get me. I wouldn't get near a window because I thought the neighbors were pointing their rifles at me and were ready to shoot me at any time. This sounds ridiculous but in my mind these thoughts seemed real. At night I thought there were people in the hallway of my house inching their way to 'get me.'

It got to the point where I was taking messages from the radio and television. Or at least I thought they were messages intended for me personally. While watching TV at noon the weather lady gestured with her thumb (as if to hitchhike) and said, "Go to Tucumcari because the weather there is perfect." I know this also sounds ridiculous, but at the time I could have sworn she was talking directly to me. I subsequently went out the front door and slowly began walking to Tucumcari.

It was the middle of June so I was walking in the blistering heat. I walked through my neighborhood along Unser Boulevard past King Road for about ten miles. At one point I picked up a bottle of discarded Power Ade I found along the way and drank it to relieve my thirst. I walked past King Road until the heat began to wear on me so I rested under a pine tree for a little while. My immediate plan was to make it to the water tank I could see at a distance and spend the night there then continue on in the morning.

I found out later that back at home my mother was looking for me but couldn't find me anywhere inside or outside the house, or in the neighborhood. She called my friend Larry, who lived close by and whom I sometimes visited, but he told her I wasn't there and that he hadn't seen me for a few days. She knew I had not been feeling well for some time and began to worry. She checked the garage and saw that both my car and her car were parked there. She also found my wallet with my ID and money on the nightstand in my room and then knew that something was not right. She called my sister in Las Cruces and told her that I was missing. She immediately called the Department of Public Safety in the city where I lived and they put out a local APB for me.

The Police Department found me at about 7:00 that evening. I had been resting under another pine tree next to the side of the road for a while. When I got up and started on my trek again three or four patrol cars with sirens blasting approached and the police promptly told me to spread-eagle on the hood of one of their cars. They frisked me, handcuffed me and held me at gunpoint. They sat my butt on the side of the road and with a gun pointed at my head asked me if I knew what time it was and I said about 3:00. Then the gung-ho policewoman with the gun in her hand yelled out its 7:00 you son-of-a-bitch! Once the police realized I was not a threat to myself or to others they removed the handcuffs and allowed one of my other sisters to approach me and give me a drink of water. They then put me in the back of an ambulance.

I now understand why that officer was so gung-ho. Only a couple of years earlier two policeman in Albuquerque were on a domestic dispute call. They were surprised by a paranoid schizophrenic individual who had a gun and killed both officers. This man also went on to kill three other innocent individuals before he was arrested. Now, all mentally ill persons have to be cautious about disclosing the fact that they are ill because the public as a whole thinks that a mentally ill person is going to 'lose it' at any minute. Many mentally ill individuals who do not take their medication, like the individual above, can be and are a problem. On their meds they begin to think that there is nothing wrong with them and are very hesitant to admit that they truly are mentally ill. Personally I was told by one of my doctors that if I didn't take my medication I would end up locked up in a psychiatric ward, destitute on the streets or even dead. That was eye opening enough for me to actually admit that I couldn't live without my meds because I truly was mentally ill. Unfortunately, there are too many schizophrenics who are unwilling to admit they are sick but fortunately I am not one of them.

On the way to the hospital I told the paramedics that after the doctor examines me and releases me I will continue on my way to Tucumcari. While in the exam room I was still fearful of others and wouldn't allow the nurse to put an I.V. in me because I thought I was going to be poisoned. It took three sisters, two nurses and about forty minutes to be convinced I was dehydrated enough to need the I.V. for fluids. Eventually blood was drawn from me also and after that the doctor had reason enough to keep me overnight.

That night I was unable to eat, sleep or drink and the following day, dressed in hospital clothing, tried to leave the hospital through an emergency exit. I managed to set off the alarm before my sister, her husband and a male nurse physically restrained me and convinced me to wait for the psychiatrist to examine me. Later I was examined and found not to be in complete control of my senses so I was transferred to the mental ward. It had been over ten years since I had been in that hospital so I knew what to expect in the mental ward. I wasn't released for another week.

While there I was exposed to other schizophrenics in much, much worse shape than me. Under medication I was back to normal and able to think straight. There was one patient especially mentally ill who inspired, (inspired is perhaps not the word to use- more like shocked) me to write the following poem:

A Different View

Everybody has a different view,
I see it red but another may not.
To another, it has a separate hue,
It could be cold or it could be hot.

For example; take the person gay,
Everyday what he must go through.
To most people life is perfectly okay,
But to a befuddle-minded few,

It must be a difficult, difficult duel.
When nature tells one what to do
And the sex drive makes another rule.
(The internal affair forces one askew.)

I knew a man who went extreme.
Difficult, so difficult what I'd seen.

He couldn't afford the proper team-
Cutoff the manhood he'd once been.

Obsessed was not the word to use-
Possessed, to throw away a person
And take the form he didn't choose.
Passion gone awry and it was done.

And of the sound heart and mind
That profess- I'll do it my way.
What God requires does not bind.
I don't care what He says- I'll stay.

Perhaps there is another concept
Can turn away that life style.
Simply accept to being inept
In self-restraint and self-denial.

Or if you declare that God loves all
And He made you what you are-
I say, open up His word and call.
You came out, now come out far.

While in the hospital I was asked by one of the patients
what would have happened to me if I had reached the water
tank? On reflection I was thinking what I would have done
and I was about forty five minutes away. During my trek I
decided not to go around the bend and follow the road to
the water tank and took a short cut through the desert itself.
I walked a mile or two through the sand and the bushes I
scared a few jackrabbits and at one point heard a crackling
noise that scared the hell out of me. I had disturbed a rattle
snake. When I realized I had almost stepped on a snake I
decided to rest under the shade of a nearby pinon tree. After

all, the threat from the dirt, the weeds, the stickers, the ants and the strange insects was no threat at all compared to a rattlesnake. While under the cool shade of the tree I took off my shoes, popped a few blisters and continued on my trek through the desert hoping to reach the water tank before dark. My plan was to spend the night on the side of the tank opposite the road where no one could see or find me. The next morning I was going to walk to Highway 550 (about 2 miles) and from there, another 2 miles to I-25 north through Santa Fe toward Denver completely unaware and unconcerned that Tucumcari was on east I-40. That is what actually did happen but what would have happened is any bodies guess- I probably would have hitchhiked north once on I-25 to who knows where.

During my hospital stay the psychiatrist advised me to apply to the Veteran Administration for benefits. The doctor's immediate concern, however, was to find me another source to provide my medication. I was referred to Pathways Inc., an agency that provides temporary psychiatric follow-up treatment and samples of medication to patients in need. That's exactly what they did for me. I was at Pathways for about a year. The attending psychiatrist there observed me closely and became aware of my complete medical history. With his help in providing the VA with the 'new evidence' they required I was awarded service connected benefits. Finally, I had a permanent and reliable source of follow-up treatment and medication for my schizophrenia.

XX

EIGHTEEN YEARS LOST

The lack of accessibility to expensive anti-psychotics is not the only reason I have nearly lost my sanity and my life. Recently I experienced an extremely stressful situation where I examined my own soundness of mind. Ever since my discharge from the military I had lived with my mother as she was living practically alone. She was elderly living on her Social Security Pension and I was on Social Security Disability Insurance. We were both happy with our living arrangement and didn't bother anyone for anything.

After living under the same roof for over 18 years I met Lena. My brother was in the process of getting a divorce after twenty three years in an unhappy marriage and was having a difficult time. He and a friend of his, who is from Mexico, were planning a trip there to do some night-clubbing. My brother told me of this trip and I decided to tag along. While in Mexico the first night we went to various night clubs, rented a hotel room to stay and my brother seemed to forget his problems for a while at least. The next day our friend took us to his brother's house and his daughter was there. I instantly fell in love

Subsequently I made many, many trips to Mexico to get to know this young lady. We got to know each other very well and she gradually fell in love with me and we eventually planned to marry. I planned on bringing her home to live with me and my mother. When my sister, who had the authority to make decisions for our mother's care under a General Durable Power of Attorney, told me "That'll never happen," all hell broke loose in our family. Four of the remaining nine of us wanted our mother to stay where she was and the other five wanted her to be put in a nursing home. Our mother was suffering from dementia and in the very early stages of Alzheimer's disease.

For me, personally, this was horrible. Imagine living with someone you love and cared for, for over eighteen years and then have that team broken up in the last quarter. On top of that she had told me many times that she doesn't want to be alone. She asked me when I was discharged from the service to stay with her as I had originally planned to move back to Grants. I had even gone to check out a house one of my cousins was selling in Grants but changed my mind when she asked me to stay with her. I wrote a poem about this during the time she was in a home and it goes as follows:

SLIPPING AWAY

I can see the tears in her eyes
And the fear in her good-byes

She knows, beyond the words she talks
She goes, beyond the door that locks

All those years together- gone
We moved from the valley to the heights

It took us from dust till dawn
I'd check the doors, the windows and lights

We even graveled the lawn
If I wasn't there she wouldn't sleep nights

And disagreements- maybe one
But I remember, there weren't any fights

Take me home…
I don't want to be here she says
Take me home...
There must be other ways
Take me home…
I need to work days
Take me home…
To where my mother stays

I won't be here tomorrow…
But I'll find you wherever you go

Can someone be so callow?...
Seems unlikely, but yes, yes it is so

Parting I say, is sad sorrow…
There is nothing I can do. I know

What time I have I borrow…
Don't you dare, don't you dare go

XXI

A SCHIZOPHRENIC WAY

And how was I able to deal with my schizophrenia during this horrendous experience? Well, the stress was worse than what I had experienced while I was in the military, in California or anywhere else. Once again I had irrational and suicidal thoughts creeping in my mind, but it would have been cowardly especially when I thought about what it would have done to my mother. I believe a suicidal person at that very moment of maximum despair must be insane. Because, when he or she is capable of the ultimate act all rationality goes by the wayside. When the only way out is oblivion- that is insanity. As I like to write poetry I wrote a poem about schizophrenia and insanity and how I resolve the problem between the two and it goes as follows:

A Schizophrenic Way

I had a thought on my mind but it went astray.
Can't figure out why I would toss a perfectly good thought.
It had something to do with a schizophrenic way,
A way of thinking that made my reasoning form into a knot.

It occasionally happens to me while I am unaware.
Unreliable images penetrate almost every single concept
In my brain to affect and distort each idea there,
Such that all reason, intellect and faculty become inept.

Let me give an example of what happens, precisely-
Total insecurity permeates the process of normal thinking.
Such that every intact notion breaks down, decidedly-
When natural chemical balances in the brain start twisting.

Everything is then unclear what constitutes reality,
And then there's a problem; every fact becomes elementary.
A very dreadful situation where the individuality
Of one becomes so confused every concept too, is imaginary.

What is primary to every schizophrenic mind-
The literal interpretation of absolutely everything as reality.
Including caricatures- not a thing is left behind.
So distorted are all thoughts they almost reach insanity.

What distinguishes one schizophrenic thought
From an insane one is that its grasp on reality will distort.
Whereas, the insane mind will definitely not.
It will completely collapse and is beyond repair of any sort.

A schizophrenic thought will easily go astray.
But an insane one cannot grasp the real from the unreal.
A mind can be retrieved in a schizophrenic way.
What I'm saying is- schizophrenia and insanity have a deal.

So it seems I have, at least in my mind and in my life, resolved my problem with mental illness. I AM mentally ill- something for many years I wasn't willing or able to admit. Something I know many seriously sick individuals are not willing to admit. Once they are able to come to the reality that they are on the brink of insanity and that there are medications nowadays that have little or no side-affects they can lead a normal life- I am proof of that.

Just as a schizophrenic individual has the capacity to pick the road he or she takes, so naturally, I do believe, does a whole society have the capacity to determine its own fate. I wrote another very short poem expressing the road our society appears to be taking. It may seem strange that a whole society can be schizophrenic but after writing this poem I am convinced that we do live in a society that is a bit schizophrenic and the road we seem to be taking is quite grim.

Awaken

The voice some humans own
Is deaf- though it reverberates
Because distant winds bleed stone.
We are numb to silent gates
That open and still remain.
The song some humans praise
Resounds a muted claim.
This, the far off echo says,
"The secret badge is quiet."
But bitter silence will be taken
And the shadows will riot
When innocence does awaken.

The voice I speak of is the current political leadership which is deaf to the cries of over a million innocent babies being slaughtered every year in this country. The voice resonates loudly as this sad, sad song is being sung. While the rhetoric of those same political leaders is so, so cold justifying the butchery (and it can only be called that- butchery) they must bleed rocks not to be in any way sensitive to what they are doing. The 'gate' I speak of is the right to legally do away with the unborn. There is no outrage, there is no one speaking out loudly enough to protect them. Those gates are open and they still remain open under the pretext of protecting, but the real reason is way beyond me to understand the ice water that must run through those veins. And I repeat that woeful song is mute as none can claim a stronger voice. The echo through the halls of government and everywhere else where this is being allowed to happen is acrimoniously quiet. The blood that spills (secret badge) will one day awaken as the shadows of all those souls innocently taken will eventually riot either through man's impatience or God's vengeance, or both (and as we all know vengeance is the Lord's).

And so a schizophrenic person (and maybe even a schizophrenic society as well) is on the road to misery, on the road to insanity or on the road to a normal life. Which road he takes is up to him. If he is willing to admit he IS mentally ill- on proper medication he will be okay. If he is not ready to accept his illness he will be miserable, or in time, even dead. If he can be 'scared straight' he can lead a normal life. I took the road that led me, at least at the moment, to a wonderful life.

XXII

A WONDERFUL LIFE

Life has never been better for me. I found and married the woman of my dreams. She had a six year old daughter when we met and we now have a son of our own. We live a quiet and peaceful life and though I am unable to work doing what I went to school and trained for I do hold a rewarding part-time job and have done so for well over fifteen years. There are the occasional minor glitches that every relationship experiences but they are usually because of my illness. For example; I occasionally have bad dreams or even nightmares that cause me to lose sleep. Recently I had a bad dream about my father and wrote a poem about it. The dream is about my overbearing father who often would denigrate my person and it goes as follows:

There is a Man

There is a man beside me
Who tells me what to do
And often where to go
He does it from a distance now
Having lost his voice and his reason
Which never was very clear
To begin with
He would often talk about his 'person'
As if he had lost it somewhere, somehow,
Because of me
But now his influence is very remote
However; strong
He grabs me from the arm as if to hit me
To throw me out of the house
But I say no- no
And run off in my own direction
His ability to tell me who I am
And what I'm worth is all very slight
Having become my own man with God's help
In my own way
Having realized my own value
As a person
And acknowledged that my merit
Never was worthless

Although it took many, many years of personal soul searching, I overcame and got over my childhood wounds. I look at an occasional bad dream as just a reminder of where I came from and it helps me to keep my bearings in the right mode for my family. The two most influential people in a person's world are generally their mother and father, and so it was in mine. My father, though supportive, was in ways also abusive but my mother was just the opposite- a friend and at times even a confidant. When she was taken away it was nothing less than solitaire for a time and I wrote a short poem about being home alone so much.

Solitaire

Me and the birds
>*Listen to the waterfall*
>*While they drink I thirst*
>*And they land on the waterfall*

While I listen
>*Even the mosquitoes drink*
>*As they congregate*
>*Round the waterfall*

While I thirst
>*The hummingbirds today*
>*Are nowhere to be found*
>*But the sparrows drink*

And my thirst continues
>*Even the bees come*
>*Looking for pollen*
>*Satisfying their need*

As my thirst persists
>*I'm hoping the rabbit*
>*Will say something*
>*As he munches in the bushes*

The situation of being alone wasn't permanent as I was soon married with an instant family to support and they keep me in loving company now. There were many years, however, when I was without a family of my own because I was unstable mentally and unable financially to support one. During those sad years there were two nephews that visited my mother (and me, I like to think) that brought a bit of warmth into my heart. In visiting us as they did and even in staying with us for a brief time while their house was being built I wrote a short poem for two of them and it goes as follows:

Isaac and Thomas

Then there is Isaac and Thomas
Sons of a sister, so much a lass

Little Ike, every bit of five
As son and brother does he thrive

And Thomas, oh my, oh my
I would, from now till I die

With infinite measures of silver
Give freely, for warming my shiver

And countless measures of gold
Send dearly, for comforting my cold

For the much Little Ike has given
Along with the love Tom has deep driven.

So well are things going for me that I began to think of what my next life would have to be like to better the one I have. I wrote another poem on just this subject. I have always wanted to be a musician and if there is a next life for me I ask that it be as follows:

Manuel Griego

In My Next Life

In my next life
I'm going to be a musician
Play the guitar like no one ever has
Eric Clapton will admire my style
I'll sing and chant with a velvety voice
"Old Blue Eyes' eyes will turn green
I'll have rhythm
Lots and lots of rhythm
I'll carry a tune anywhere
It wants to go
And I'll write songs everyone
Will hear and appreciate
The Lennon/McCartney Duo
Will blush with admiration
When they hear my lyrics
They will have such rhyme and reason
And intellectual proficiency that
Their poetic content will be infallible
In my next life
Music will be my calling
Any instrument I choose to play
Will capitulate as I require
The saxophone will mourn or leap
For joy at will in my hands
The piano will surrender it's keys
Willingly as it has never before
There will be hordes and hordes of
Fans wanting to hear me
And all my songs
I will be honored by the Lord Himself
To play the trumpet

At his return
My harp playing will be so foreboding
That no one will want
To touch another harp ever again
Yes, in my next life
Music will be so prevalent
That it will be the only form
Of communication and
If you can't sing a happy song
You can't commune with
The spirit of the soul
So you might as well not
Plan on coming to my world
Since angels cannot sing
Until redemption is complete
THAT will be my task
In my next life-
To entertain, to inform
To interact with my
Musical prowess
Until all receive their just rewards
I will, with my musical adeptness
Be in control
So pray you all believe as I do
So you can hear me sing, play
Compose and
Conduct in my next life

All is well in paradise today and it got even better when I learned that I was going to be a father for the first time. Although the delivery gave us a very real scare everything turned out just fine, such that I wrote a poem for my son:

Manuel Griego

A Father's Advice

There is in our family a new born- our first.
A full month early into the world he came.
A prayer alone saved them from the hearse.
Holding on tightly he forever made his claim
And with him came the grandest of thirst.

Less than five pounds is what he weighed.
(Four pounds and two ounces to be exact),
A full forty eight centimeters long he laid,
With fingers and toes and all senses intact
As all night long, I so anxiously prayed.

Now, safe and sound at home he lay
And cries only when his appetite wakes-
To him, it's all the same- night and day.
And I'll do within reason whatever it takes
To make sure his dreams don't go astray.

Tonight, as I write this poem in the den,
He lay quietly in crib with mother nearby.
And I hope that for him many doors open.
The one most of Interest to me is up high,
So, I'll tell my dear son; we are just men.

We come and we go and we do as we please
Until the time comes when we go eye to eye
With the One above; then we get on our knees.
So, if something to me happens and soon I die
From what I understand these are the keys:

If you can, take your neighbor by the hand,
(It seems much, but it's such a small world).

All want a pass by and by to the promise land,
So, I leave you to make the planet unfurled,
And of your generation; just take command.

It's a suitable challenge I know you can meet.
Now second of all; do not forget your maker-
Not me, no certainly not me, and I do repeat
Not me. But The One to whom you will answer.
He will guide you and make all things complete.

And third; on your journey take with you,
(As wisdom is best shown through quietude),
A reposeful posture towards everything you do
And avoid a boisterous and obtrusive attitude.
Oh, and of your shot- always follow through.

We are now at a point where we have outgrown our abode. Not physically or financially- because there's only four of us, but spiritually. We like our neighborhood and our neighbors and our house is quite adequate for our needs. But we need a change of climate and a change of environment and we think the best place for us is to move to the country. Way out in the country- literally the mountains. We think it would be best to raise our children where external influences are not so strong, where they can learn about nature by being very close to it. We think they will have a life time to get in touch with society. So naturally I wrote a poem about making a move.

Hunger

Should I move or should I stay?
Don't know what to do at this moment.
I could very easily be on my way.
If I go, then comes an acknowledgement-

Manuel Griego

That I must leave all things behind
Shall I go ahead and put out a sign?
The neighbors too, have all been kind.
Shall I do like the rest and fall in line?

The quest for better is every ones search.
About what I have I can't complain,
But the view from a higher perch,
Well, it's just not the same if I remain.

Then again, how does better measure?
Does it always come with a higher price?
Of that, I'm not at all that sure.
I mean, what I have is quite nice.

And what I have I'm not about to lose.
It's free and clear, with such little debt.
I'm free to come and go as I choose
And don't want to move then regret.

But now I've seen a much nicer place.
It's given me a strangely restless mind.
I must admit I too am in the rat race.
Something I thought I'd left behind.

Now too, I've come to face a certain reality.
As much of the world starves for a meal
I ask- have I come to complete insanity?
All I'm thinking is- can I get a good deal?

And as for my family, as all things are considered, we serve the Lord first and believe because of it are rich in happiness and in many other ways as well. My struggle with schizophrenia is by no means over. I deal with paranoia, anxiety and feelings of guilt from time to time. Not to mention voices, thoughts of suicide, messages from the radio and television that disrupt my thinking and now a very slight inability to relate to people. These symptoms of schizophrenia I have learned to fight off, and deal with them on an ongoing basis, but I have certainly resolved the problem of isolation.

My condition, experts say, is a chemical imbalance inside my brain but as long as I have a reliable source of medication, follow-up treatment and a stable life without excessive stress I can and will continue to overcome this affliction I live with. It is chronic and although it seems to a few individuals that I currently know who see me function so well that I am not at all schizophrenic. I too, at times, am tempted to think the same, but I do not have the courage to go without my medication for even one day because I know what will happen to me after a short time. I have for years been on the highest dose of Abilify that doctors recommend and am very cautiously being put on a lower dose. Potentially there are long term side effects to being on such a high dose and it is thought that if I can possibly function as well on a lower dose I should.

This, the fourth book I am proud to have written, hopefully will provide some insight to others who suffer from schizophrenia and in some small way serve as an inspiration for them to continue to fight this cruel, cruel illness until the battle is won. The battle, it must be understood is day-to-day. If that is not known about schizophrenia it will certainly be a much, much more difficult road to follow. Everyone is on a road to somewhere and if one suffers from a mental illness it is best to know in what direction they are headed. The signs at first are not so easy to read because they are at some distance but once they are in sight and clearly read the road itself will either be very, very difficult or very simple to follow. Personally I am familiar with both directions. For well over twenty years I followed the thick-headed road and got nowhere, always denying and unwilling to admit the obvious- that I was mentally ill. Now I am on the road that leads somewhere. I am on a road that as you can see, lets me think straight and dream dreams that are realistic. I can't say that I wasted all those years because if I hadn't lived them I wouldn't be where I am today. That is, I wouldn't be the man that I am today, willing to want to give more than I take and actually having something worthwhile to offer to anyone who wants to listen.

My sincere hope is that what I have written in this book will do someone out there some good. Even if it is just one person- maybe that one person will not have to spend a significant amount of valuable time of his or her life to learn the lessons I learned. This is what I learned about schizophrenia: (or practically any mental illness for that matter) that I had to actually admit that I was going insane, that I was almost there- at the point of no return. After literally pulling the hair out of my head and holding a rifle under my chin and an instant away from the ultimate act, I learned that I was still sane enough to realize that I was almost insane. I mean, you have to be almost insane to try to kill yourself. It's not a question of wanting attention- it's a question of really needing attention, the right kind of attention. I was lucky enough to get attention from professionals, from friends, from loved ones, from God and from strangers. If I had only admitted that I was sick much, much sooner I wouldn't have needed to bother so many people. And so here I thank all of those people- from my parents to the doctors to the strangers and to anyone else who deliberately or inadvertently lent me a hand. Thank You, I say again Thank You.

In closing I want to add one more poem that justifies my whole purpose in writing not only this book but the other books I have written and God willing will also write in the future. It explains my philosophy and gives me reason to want to better the world in any way I possibly can. Hopefully, those of you who read the book enjoyed it and I sincerely hope that your time and money was well spent.

What Has This Pen?

What has this pen
To drip upon this page?
Who is this man
To think himself a sage?

And of this paper
What has it to say?
Is this some caper
To save another day?

Ink and sheet- the gall!
Why peruse every word?
What care you all
If this poem is ever heard?

This is just another man
Trying only to be brave
Asking everything he can
Before they dig his grave.

THE END